THE COURAGE TO CHOOSE

THE COURAGE TO CHOOSE

⋙⋙⋙ *An American Nun's Story* ⋘⋘⋘

By *MARY GRIFFIN*

LITTLE, BROWN AND COMPANY
BOSTON · TORONTO

T 08/75

FIRST EDITION

The author is grateful for permission to reprint the following previously published material:
Lines from "Heaven Haven" and "The Wreck of the Deutschland" by Gerard Manley Hopkins. Reprinted by permission of Oxford University Press from *Poems of Gerard Manley Hopkins*, Oxford University Press, 1948. "Poverty" by Judy Washbush, which appeared in the October, 1972, issue of *Sisters Today*. Published by St. John's Abbey, Collegeville, Minnesota.

Library of Congress Cataloging in Publication Data

Griffin, Mary Annarose, Sister.
  The courage to choose.

  Autobiographical.
  Includes bibliographical references.
  1. Griffin, Mary Annarose, Sister.   2. Monastic
and religious life of women.   3. Ex-nuns—Personal
narratives.   I. Title.
BX4705.G62245A33   271'.91   [B]   75-9636
ISBN 0-316-32864-2

Designed by Janis Capone

*Published simultaneously in Canada
by Little, Brown & Company (Canada) Limited*
PRINTED IN THE UNITED STATES OF AMERICA

To Jane, to Donatus, to all my sisters beginning with Marion

PREFACE

This book grew out of my attempt to confront my own experience and to discover its meaning. An attempt, essentially, to understand my own nature, as well as the cultural and spiritual climate which largely accounts for me.

Vatican Council II, convoked by Pope John XXIII in 1962, called on the entire Catholic world to undertake an *aggiornamento,* to bring itself fully into the twentieth century. The renewal efforts with which American nuns responded changed the shape of our lives and generated a moral imperative to make sense of the past. Like Faulkner's Quentin Compson, the history-obsessed protagonist of *The Sound and the Fury,* many felt a painful and immediate urgency to try to "save" the past. Those who could not sometimes fell victim to an unhappy cynicism which led them to focus only on the dark side of the ambiguity of experience.

Although I could not preserve my own past intact, I found myself looking back not with a sigh but with a mixture of surprise, fascination, and laughter, coupled with gratitude for all that juice and all that joy.

The past is not only prologue. It is a living force in the present. I have tried to re-create it in all its vitality, all its frustrating, frequently wrongheaded but always engaging complexity. American nuns have transformed the local color of their lives almost beyond belief. But all of us, those who left and those who stayed, carry our pre–Vatican II formation in our bones. Deep-rooted values, patterns of thought, vestiges of ritual cling to us still. The chapel may indeed be bare, the sweet birds flown, but what is of the essence remains: commitment, community, Christianity.

August 5, 1974
NEW YORK CITY

CONTENTS

THE COURAGE TO CHOOSE

WHY THEY WENT

A standpoint . . . is a complex of all those things
that compose an inquiring who.
— MICHAEL NOVAK
Ascent of the Mountain, Flight of the Dove

Benjamin De Mott describes it accurately: "You wake up on the morning of a new decade resolved to explain to yourself as clearly as you can what exactly happened during the ten-year night before and you can't say a word." Why did we enter the convent? Why in the forties and fifties did American girls by the thousands turn their shoulder-length bobs on life, kick off their saddle shoes, and disappear into novitiates over the length and breadth of the land?

Why? We weren't children of alienation, turned off by a war, by hash or acid, by any kind of counterculture. We weren't seeking a simpler life; we weren't even looking for transcendental meditation (that we were expected to meditate for one half hour every morning came to most of us as a distinct shock). We had no intuition of a "milennialism" looming on the American horizon. We had little sense of collective or personal guilt. If anything, we tended toward a kind of triumphalism. We did have a deep concern for the welfare of others. And we felt specially graced, "called" to the service of others for the sake of the Kingdom.

The sense of being "called" is what the church termed the *grace of vocation*. Catholic children began to assimilate this bit of theology at the first frightening encounter with the kindergarten Sister, swathed from head to toe in awesome black, or with Father at the church door on Sunday morning, sporting his long buttoned skirt and his funny three-cornered hat. These were people "who belong to God, darling." They lived in God's house. And wasn't that wonderful?

Eventually young Catholics absorbed the official explanation — the grace of vocation. You were "called" to a life of poverty, chastity, and obedience. And that call was so compelling that at eighteen, at twenty, you could say a final, sweeping no to the possibility of an exclusive human love; no to children and a home of your own; in some cases no to a career toward which you were tending. This in order to say a final ringing yes to a total and permanent identification with Christ who had mysteriously singled you out for Himself. "You have not chosen me, but I have chosen you," the postulant would be reminded. And in a way that fact made it a whole lot easier. It explained rationally how one could "enter," hating the very idea. That Christ might have had equally little enthusiasm for the reluctant brides who each September presented themselves at the doors of Mount Carmel was an insight mercifully spared those of us who found the whole notion pretty distasteful. You weren't expected to *like* having Abraham plunge the knife in. You were just expected not to sink your teeth into his wrist as the blade approached!

Of course there were radiant candidates, flung, as it were, into the arms of the novitiate on surging waves of religious fervor. Sitting up in bed in the chilly autumn nights, hugging my flannel-gowned knees as I tried for the hundredth time to figure out what in the world I was doing in the convent, I would remember the faces of the postulants I was sure belonged — the fervent ones. The ones who really kept the silence, knelt straight as ramrods through morning meditation, lowered their shocked eyes when you tilted your water basin crazily over one eye like a World War I doughboy as you were waiting in line for water after night prayers. I stole stealthy glances into those faces each evening as I finished saying the Stations. I could safely do so, for their eyes were riveted on the crucifix — adoring, defenseless eyes. And I would mask my own and turn aside, feeling somehow that I was intruding — knowing that such moments of rapt prayerful intimacy were totally outside my experience. I could *will* to serve. But I couldn't make myself like it. The sweetness, the ardor of novice voices singing "O cor amoris victima" touched me. But the words vaguely embarrassed me. They struck me as sentimental and I fled with relief to the organ loft where I could grapple with pedals and stops instead of devotional hymns.

No one ever acts from a single motive, of course. Undoubtedly there were wheels within wheels for all of us. And undoubtedly many of our motives were hidden from ourselves. The novitiate had to attract some neurotic personalities fleeing personal freedom. There were always the few looking for a refuge, escaping an impossible home or an importunate boyfriend or the paralyzing prospect of not marrying at all! But usually these immature few didn't last. Vicki dissolved into tears two weeks after we'd arrived, fished out the engagement ring she kept tucked in her underskirt pocket, and sobbed that she was going home. One irate father arrived with a warrant and spirited away the single wealthy postulant among us. Even I had my moment of romantic relief when the guy I had shunted off on a partner who seemed made for him showed up at Mount Carmel after her funeral, having crashed the car on their honeymoon. To him it was a sign that he should have married me after all. To me, a sign that I'd better dig out my old address book fast before the Novice Mistress caught on to the purpose of that visit.

My own deepest motivation was not, I suspect, very doctrinal. I did not see myself as a Bride of Christ, one to whom Christ had given Himself totally and who could do nothing other than respond with as total a gift of self. I felt, in fact, thoroughly uncomfortable with such a notion. My life had been singularly devoid of what William James would have termed religious experience. (In the third grade I had cried out loud and had to be quieted when the Dominican preaching the children's mission gave too graphic an account of the crucifixion. But that was the end of that.) I was willing to forego marriage, but not because I felt spiritually espoused and had no normal attractions. I was quite hung up on an atheistic medical student at the University of Chicago who had written in exasperation, "It's me or that nutty idea of yours. You decide." I was willing to be poor, to try to be obedient, to remain unmarried for the sake of the Kingdom — to spread the Gospel of Christ, to be an extension of His concern for all men. I didn't expect to be happy doing this. But I did expect to be useful, to bring a more significant happiness to others. If Freud was right, my relations with God reflected those with my father. Both were distant, awe-inspiring, admirable, austere, and no at all accessible to human affection. Like my approach to my father, my approach to God was overwhelmingly cognitive.

Through half a dozen Ignatian retreats I had heard the call of the Master, "Come follow me." Jesuit spirituality sped arrowlike to my receptive mind. In the meditation on the Two Standards, I un-hesitatingly chose the Standard of Christ. When we contemplated the Three Classes of Men, I knew that I should throw in my lot with the young man who sold all and went in poverty to follow Christ. By the time that Christ the Leader was proposed to my mesmerized gaze, I was irretrievably lost. I *would* be one of that "army of youth," bearing the standards of truth and fighting for Christ the Lord. That master psychologist, Ignatius of Loyola, spoke as unerringly to me as to Francis Xavier: "What doth it profit a man to gain the whole world and suffer the loss of his eternal soul?" In the hushed chapel, the sanctuary lamps flickering in their amber cut-glass bowls, the incense of Benediction spiraling upward, the retreat master facing us gravely across the gleaming wooden table inside the gilt-edged sanctuary gate — in that otherworldly atmosphere everything seemed possible: to give and not to count the cost, to say generously, "Take and receive." It took eight years — four high school retreats, four in college. But the resolve finally stuck. I wasn't very heroic that August night when I determined to enter. If I wanted to make the break, I had to do it swiftly or my shaky nerve would collapse. At breakfast on August 23 I released the news to my stunned family. On September 8 (without even a chilly farewell from my father and sister who had barely spoken to me in the intervening days) I opened the front door a final time, took the "El" to Wilmette, and drove to Dubuque with a classmate who was entering with me. And when the doors of the motherhouse closed behind me that evening I felt that I'd drawn my last free breath in this life. But I knew deep down inside that I was doing what God had all along planned that I should do. And I felt the peace of having at last decided.

It was so irrefutably rational, this choice. All the bits and pieces of my life fitted snugly together in a beautifully logical mosaic. I felt *cosmically* right. Happiness was ephemeral: truth was for all time. To find my life I must lose it. This was the first truth to quench my insatiable appetite for meaning. And I felt it with singular force as the whole truth of my being.

As I think about it now, two facets of the situation strike me as significant. One is the astonishing privateness of the experience. I was wholly incapable of explaining myself to anyone. The other is the enormous influence on me of the nuns who had surrounded my entire school life. Whether or not, as Sandra Schneider suggests, they passed on to me some of their "compulsions, complexes, and practical heresies,"* for good or for ill they dominated my young years beyond all telling. And I identified with them ardently.

No one who did not experience a middle-class Catholic childhood in twentieth-century America can be expected to understand what this latter experience was like. The nuns of my growing-up years were a unique experience. I feel genuine nostalgia when I think about those days. And I feel sorry for all the Catholic youngsters who will have to grow up outside the kind of parochial school experience the nuns provided.

Sister Cyprianna was my introduction to the Sisterhood. Her domain was the first-grade classroom in the tiny parish school we lived near in Chicago. Ageless she seemed to me then; now I guess that she was well past retirement age but still going strong. Pale, indeed white-faced, shapeless, with rimless glasses crammed into her bonnet, Sister Cyprianna reigned like a semibenevolent tyrant. She could be cajoled into reading us stories. But woe betide the wriggling torso, the scraping foot of an inattentive first-grader. A warning would in justice be given. But a second offense meant immediate banishment to the darkness of the enormous cloakroom. There, in a lonely forest of galoshes, a wilderness of woolen scarfs and linked mittens, the exile served out her sentence, separated from the tantalizing story in progress, cut off from the sudden bursts of laughter, and — worst of all — an outcast from the milk break, when great glass bottles of Bowman Dairy chocolate milk rattled

---

* Sandra M. Schneider, I.H.M., *The Theological Significance of Virginity According to the Fathers of the First Three Centuries.* Unpublished dissertation submitted to the Institut de Catholique de Paris, June, 1971, pp. 52–53.

invitingly in the hands of the blessed who had not sinned. Rainy days were the most deliciously terrifying of all. When the thunder burst in the sky and the rain streamed down the huge classroom windows, when it grew so dark that the classroom lights had to be put on though it was only mid-morning, then it was that the nether world came at Sister Cyprianna's behest and great dark angels stood broodingly about waiting to pounce on any foolish first-grader who spoke at the pencil sharpener or poked the invitingly bared bottom of the boy in front of one who had forgotten to button up after he'd been to the boys' washroom. More than once, a public sinner, I had to move to one side of my tiny desk to let the Dark Angel sit beside me: I so obviously wanted his company!

Sister Nativity captivated us in third grade. To say that we adored her is vastly to understate the situation. My brother Philip confessed that he loved her madly. So did Henry Myskins and Nicholas Ishkum, I'm sure. And I knew in my heart that Sister Nativity was the most beautiful creature in the whole world. One lugged cartons to school, clapped erasers until the chalk dust coated one's navy blue uniform, polished the shining front of the classroom to a glasslike finish Mop and Glow will never approach, even begged for the privilege of washing the basement windows of the convent on Saturday morning — all because this brown-eyed, laughing young Sister was on the receiving end of such mighty attentions. Tall, slim, with a graceful liquid walk that rivaled the silken movements of Herrick's Julia, Sister Nativity was the antithesis of dried-up little Cyprianna. Silent reading, drawing, arithmetic — those were magic hours that no one ever wanted to end. The third grade worshiped its unashamed idol, burned its incense, and struggled to school on May mornings with armloads of backyard flowers. For Sister Nativity the entire class turned up daily at 7:30 Mass. Not rain, nor sleet, nor icy blast, not even the scent of pancakes sizzling on the griddle could detain the pure in heart from darting down the street as the church bell sounded. Sister would be waiting. That was reward enough. A dozen vocations to the priesthood budded on the boys' side of the room. Every little girl in the class secretly tried on a turkish towel to see if, veiled, she would look the least bit like Her. Sister Nativity enchanted the minds and hearts of the lucky third grade. There could never be another.

And yet there were others — sharp-tempered old Cleophas was fat and had "big lungs" and smelled bad and hit the boys over the head with a tin-edged ruler. There was Benignus of the black eyes and rapier wit who taught us piano and borrowed murder mysteries from our fathers; Orestes in seventh grade, standing with one hand on her hip, the other brandishing Dubbs's *Mental Arithmetic* as she charged into the daily battle of numbers, our straggly little lines dashing haphazardly after her, on fire with the challenge of beating Dubbs in his own field.

Orestes was the Boys' Teacher. It was understood without resentment that she didn't care much for girls. She trained the altar boys. She coached the eighth-grade candidates for Quigley, the minor seminary. She taught them English and a smattering of algebra and saw that they were letter-perfect in catechism and Bible history. And they rewarded her efforts by carrying off the lion's share of the scholarships to Quigley and came back a year or two after graduation to visit her in her classroom, craning their necks out of tight collars, running their hands self-consciously over pimply young chins, flaunting their first long trousers and their Latin books. Eventually some of them made it through to ordination and they never forgot Sister Orestes, who had "awakened" their vocations and who turned up at the cathedral with handmade burses or satin stoles or breviaries the superior had supplied for "Orestes' boys." The Eighth-Grade Sister — a thousand priests must look back on her proselytizing with wry smiles of amusement, with admiration for her fierce recruiting ability, with affection for her unswerving devotion to "her boys."

But it was in high school where the girls found their métier — the Catholic girls' central high school, the private boarding academy, the convent school for young ladies — islands of femaleness where (save for the janitor, the retreat master, and the band director) the Second Sex was first. And love, when it burgeoned, meant having a "case" on the senior class president, or a wild attachment to the third year Latin teacher. Whatever teaching assignments the provincial made to the grade schools (there had to be a good "boys' teacher" and a superior who could get along with the pastor), she deployed her forces to the community-run high school with a genius an employment agency would envy. In her prime, Miss Jean Brody viewed each class as the "crème de la crème." Marshaling her faculty for the girls' high school, the provincial chose her own crème de la crème. The nuns were young (later I realized that some were still in their teens), they were bright (most of them working for master's degrees at local universities on top of full-time teaching schedules), they were brimming with laughter and love of life, and they *adored* their students. Even when they wanted to kill us with their bare hands, they went on loving us for the sake of God, suffering adolescents patiently, and endearing themselves to generations of Catholic girls who cannot think of their youth without remembering the delicious nuns who wove themselves along with their ideals permanently into the lives of their charges.

The incomparable Sister Emilita came with high school. A thousand blue-serged, black-stockinged girls rising with one mighty swoosh at the lift of Sister Emilita's baton. The sweet dark altos begin, "Ce-ci-lia o-o-o-o-or-*ga*-nis." Voice after voice enters — second alto, soprano, until a thousand young voices ring out the ageless polyphony of "Hymn to St. Cecilia." Then the school song sung to the appropriated strains of Schubert's "March Militaire": "To our high school each one of us will be true. To our high school loyal we'll be through and through." And finally the school hymn, "Immaculata, alma ma-a-ter, we give our he-arts to you." Wherever they are across this world, Immaculata girls, I am certain, can stand and sing every word as if it were yesterday and they were transfixed beneath Sister Emilita's magic hand.

Music bound our days together. The famed Noble Cain himself came to direct the Glee Club (and stayed to shock us with a few mighty *damn*'s when our diminuendo failed to descend to a whisper). He got the effects he was working toward with us. But we felt inchoately that it was really Sister Emilita who should have been out there in the auditorium receiving the plaudits. *She* did all the rehearsing. But *he* took all the bows. Of course, the nuns couldn't appear in public. That was their Rule. As it was the Rule that they never ate with us or came to our homes or *ever* revealed their own names or ages. And we understood all this. We undertook the most Herculean research to dredge up the romantic pasts of our favorites ("Did you know that she went *here* to school? She must be hanging in alumna corridor. Let's look!"). No scrap of information was too mean to be savored and carefully passed along ("I *know* she's only twenty-four; she went to school with Ann Ellen's cousin!"). And occasionally (oh heaven of heavens) when we stayed after school just to talk, Sister might betray her fondness with a quick little hug, a hand held a moment at the side door as she left for "Prayers" at the convent. And Janet or Ann or Eleanor, drifting blissfully busward, found herself wondering about her own generosity to Christ. If Sister could give up so much, what about her? Was that still little voice she kept repressing really the beginning of a vocation? Ought she to mention it to Sister Rosemarie the next time there was a chance for a talk?

There were, of course, the "types," the girls who "hung around" the nuns. You suspected that they might "have a vocation." But sometimes they surprised everyone by going to business school or to college and then turning up married at the very first chance. And there were always the others — the ones you'd never guess. The ones who ran the school and wrote for the paper and dated the boys from St. George's and Loyola Academy and suddenly amazed everyone by "entering." And there would be excited whispers and deep hurts for best friends who had never guessed and now felt suddenly betrayed; for a "vocation" was essentially a very private affair.

Today young people flock together into the Jesus movement, openly proclaiming their devotion to Christ, their longing for His coming, their certainty that His truth makes the difference between nothingness and reality. In the thirties we had our Cisca, our Sodality meetings and projects. They were under the direction and influence of charismatic priests like Jesuits Daniel Lord and Martin Carrabine. These were "lay" organizations, meant to leaven society with young Catholics who lived lives patterned on the moral ideas of Christianity. They were seed ground for young Catholic intellectuals like Jim O'Gara, Ed Marciniak, John Cogley. Important as Cisca was, however, it ranked second to the seminary, the novitiate. That was where the really dedicated young Catholics were pointed — the ones who felt called to give their lives totally and forever to the service of Christ in the Church.

But how could you know if you really had a vocation? The question anguished generations of committed young people. No deeper scrutiny ever preoccupied Jonathan Edwards's eighteenth-century congregation searching their hearts for signs of conversion than that which Catholic boys and girls undertook trying to determine God's will for them. It wasn't, they knew, a question to be examined lightly. One could not without risk reject the grace of a vocation.

Who could be certain that the rich young man of the Gospel had after all been saved? The official teaching of the Church was clear: if you were in good health, had no impediment (e.g., a divorce in the family, illegitimate birth), and were accepted by the religious congregation or the bishop, you *had* a vocation. But what was *not* clear was the preliminary action which brought you to the seminary or the novitiate in the first place.

In my own case, after endless hours of wavering and compromise, after deciding for and then against, after getting engaged and breaking it off, I realized one hot August night that the fact that I *saw* so clearly the rationality of a life patterned after Christ's — never mind the fact that I hated the prospect of what was entailed — this insight itself must *be* the grace. The fact that this image of life was fringed not with joy but with reluctance merely pointed to its authenticity. It was an image of sacrifice, not of celebration — or at best the celebration of a sacrifice. Significantly, it was the death days of its martyrs which the Church celebrated! Viewed from the standpoint of the generous ideals of youth, dropping one's net on the shore to follow a penniless, solitary Christ was an exhilarating notion. It was risky; if you stopped to think about it, it was quite terrifying really. It was a leap into the dark. It had about it an ineluctable finality. One knew that ages and ages hence this choice of the road less traveled would indeed have made all the difference.

For me the sharpest loss would be the chance of realizing a deep personal human relationship. This lost, nothing else mattered much. I could smile scornfully at my sister-in-law's horror over giving up crepe de chine underwear and silk stockings for cotton stuff and floor-length black serge. My father pierced straight to the heart of the matter, drawing me down beside his pillow and asking, "Can you be happy, baby, without being married?" No, not really. But I could bring a deeper, lasting happiness into the lives of others. And wasn't that much more important than one's own personal happiness? Yet, as hope of deliverance from this vision sank within me, how I yearned for a voice from Heaven halting Abraham's blade as it moved inexorably nearer. Why on earth me? Unheroic, ordinary me? As always, my anguished question trailed off into silence.

Why *not* me? the silence implied. In the end I took that question for answer. Would I be so haunted by this tantalizing invitation if Someone Up There weren't actively pursuing me? Like Francis Thompson, I fled Him down the nights and down the days. And in the labyrinthine passageways of my own heart I too tried to evade those strong feet following after. Finally, at bay, I too turned and yielded. I couldn't say yes happily: I would at least say it generously. Without a word to anyone — afraid that I'd weaken unless I acted at once — I sat at my father's rolltop desk, wrote the letter, walked to the corner mailbox, and dropped it in. It was August 22, 1939, and I felt that it was the most momentous night of my life.

In retrospect this is the way it was for me. And perhaps (since surely my experience was not unique) for some, even many, others. The nuns were, undoubtedly, the most powerful living force in our lives. Not only were they our cultural heroines, but their lives constituted an almost irresistible invitation in an essentially closed society. No more than the young of the sixties and the seventies could we of the thirties escape our time: the images it offered us, the heroes it admired. Brought up in a totally Catholic milieu, we were on the whole docile. We absorbed doctrine. We conformed. We tried deliberately to live a life focused not on this but on the next world. Thomas Merton would be our beckoning star, not Teilhard de Chardin. It was Thomas More we emulated (the King's good servant but first our Lord's). Luther we ignored. We didn't dream of changing our world. We only dreamed of saving it. Ours was not the best of all possible worlds. But it was a rational, ordered, essentially well-intentioned universe under the aegis of a good, loving Father who had but to be known to be adored. We were, after all, average Americans — innocent, messianic, insular, naïve, full of goodwill. For thousands of us, religious life appeared as our inescapable manifest destiny. We had been singularly blessed. And to whom much is given, of them much is demanded. Noblesse oblige.

Yet, from another perspective, this is not the story at all. It was much less rational and clean and tight. It included all kinds of untidy pieces, loose ends that resist being shoved into place. There were a thousand irrational impulses, feelings that won't hold still for analysis. There rush to mind a dozen influences not accounted for in such a version as this. But on the whole it is an honest account. And it is the best story I can tell myself at the moment, poised as I am on this plateau of my life from which I can at last survey the road I've taken. It will have to do for the present.

CHAPTER TWO

TAKING THE VEIL IN CATHOLIC AMERICA

Bare ruined choirs where late the sweet birds sang.
— SHAKESPEARE
Sonnet LXXIII

The night I entered the novitiate of the Sisters of Charity of the Blessed Virgin Mary I felt that I was moving backward in time to some magic country where nothing would ever change. In a certain sense I felt that my life was ending. I knew there would be work. I knew there would be prayer. I'd been told there would be austerity and discipline and an inevitable loneliness as one sought to unite oneself perfectly to the will of God.

Yet the dispatch with which we postulants were channeled through entrance formalities and whisked into the nuns' refectory for a marvelous cold supper suggested not the chilly remoteness of cloister but opening day of the new term in boarding school. What I remember vividly are the healthy appetites with which we demolished stacks of homemade bread and piles of thinly sliced ham. Afterwards the forty-seven of us crowded up the narrow pine stairs for Benediction. Hurriedly we whispered names and origins ("Terrific — another

Californian!"), laughing the bright hectic laughter of the young who must not cry, aware of a rising sense of excitement and adventure. Perhaps this was not the end at all, but the beginning of something strange and new and wonderful.

The BVM Motherhouse was pure Victoriana from its red plush bishop's parlor to its high drafty corridors lined with portraits of ancient mothers general and punctuated here and there with clumps of fern, a life-sized bronze crucifix, a Virgin wrapped in marble. But the chapel was a surprise: a bright spacious expanse arched over by a deep blue ceiling. It was refreshingly unencumbered, marred only by three white wooden altars with gingerbready spires and conventional statues. Its silence struck a hush into the postulants and we tried vainly to soften the clatter of high heels down the long polished aisles. A waning September sun filtered bluely through an old-fashioned stained-glass Madonna, incense rose in a bright cloud, and a sinuous Gregorian melody sprang toward the gold monstrance now in place. "A-do-re-mus in aeternum." It floated away to the merest whisper, then rolled back over the bowed heads of the professed nuns in a tremulous legato. And in that moment, which hangs still in my memory like some long-remembered luminous jewel, the new life began.

Later, during choir practice, I discovered the unsuspected nuts and bolts that riveted together that enchanting bridge of song. "Arcis-thesis, Sisters. Arcis-thesis. Linkers and breathers, remember. We must sustain the tone without a seam." Plump little Sister Roselle rocked back and forth on her shiny-toed shoes in what we laughingly termed her "liturgical movement."

Aching from dormitory scrubbing, sweating in long-sleeved black poplin habits, the postulants stifled their boredom and for the nth time undertook the sweet-somber Ambrosian Gloria they would sing at Reception the following March when, the initial six months of candidacy past, they would themselves receive at the hands of the archbishop the "holy habit of religion."

The night before, I knew, they would cut our hair in preparation for the close-fitting veil. Then at last we would be novices, with serge skirts and twelve-inch-wide sleeves, and lily-seed rosaries hanging from the narrow leather cinctures at our waists. At the moment we were curiously in-between, rather like girl acolytes in ankle-skimming skirts and short capes that swung open to reveal young high bosoms still encased in worldly Maidenforms. Our shoulder-length hair bounced and shone as we climbed rickety ladders to high-dust the spotless postulate. Our fingers reddened and cracked, peeling their way through a thousand bushels of green apples, new potatoes, carrots. Our tender knees sprouted protective scabs as they shifted from scrubbing pad to wooden kneeler in an already boring rhythm.

We rose at five in the chilly November mornings, splashed in the icy water that had stood all night on our bedside commodes, fought back sleep during pre-Mass meditation, fitting into the ancient novitiate routine of work and study and prayer aimed at perfection. This was our boot training. We were learning how to become nuns, how to strip away the last remnants of our vain, worldly selves. "Ora et labora" announced an ornate little motto in the postulate. And I began to realize that for me at least the two were indistinguishable.

Contrary to all the holy cards I had garnered through a Catholic girlhood in a parochial school — cards depicting a nightgowned child knocking insistently at a little gold tabernacle door, the Apostles and our Lady gazing ecstatically heavenward as tiny tongues of flame leaped above their heads, or the "Little Flower" fondling her crucifix though a coverlet of roses — prayer, I discovered, was tedious. Prayer was hard. Prayer was, to be honest, a one-sided bore. And, I found to my horror, nuns were expected not only to pray for interminably long hours (meditation at six, Mass at seven, examen at noon, a "Visit" to the Blessed Sacrament at two, spiritual reading at eight, and night prayers at eight-thirty), they were expected to live always in the presence of God.

They fell asleep in Solemn Silence with God on their minds and woke up with God on their lips. The rising prayer, said aloud in company with the other novices in your dormitory, made certain that the day's first spoken word was in praise of God. I recall that first morning when I woke at dawn to the chilling clank of metal rings being swept along curtain rods as the novices emerged from their alcoves, their high-pitched sleep-filled voices announcing, "In the name of our Lord Jesus Christ crucified, I rise from this bed of sleep. On the last day may I rise to everlasting happiness." Months later I would one morning electrify the inmates of Holy Angels dormitory with my own inaccurate but anguished version of the rising prayer. "In the name of our Lord Jesus Christ crucified, I rise from this bed of happiness. On the last day may I rise to everlasting sleep!" The heinous crime of provoking hilarity during Solemn Silence brought me to the Postulant Mistress. And she brought me to my knees.

Back in the thirties, when entrance groups of sixty-five and seventy were not unheard of, a very shrewd Mother General had named Sister Mary Angelice as Postulant Mistress. Fortyish, with liquid brown eyes that could be alarmingly stern or wickedly funny, she was a natural for her job. After fifteen years as prefect in a high-school-girls' boarding school, she played on us like an organist on his keyboard. College graduates, high school dropouts, she lumped us together with an endearing, "Children." In a joyless world of starch and silence, she was an oasis of delight. Long before we had arrived on the scene, she had painstakingly done her homework on each new postulant. So when the storm broke — as break it must during those first harrowing weeks of incarceration — she was ready for us.

Her knowing gaze fixed on the red-eyed postulant worrying a convent handkerchief across the desk from her, Sister Angelice ran through her roles in a stunning repertoire.

Now, long years later, piecing together a thousand fragmentary conversations, I begin to perceive the scope of her art. She could be confessor ("Well, why not tell me about John? It might make it easier"), spiritual guide ("You don't *have* to feel that God is listening; you just have to will yourself to pray. You must *want* to want to"), fellow conspirator ("Here, don't ask me where I got it; just thank your stars that it's Bristol Cream sherry"), friend ("I screamed when I read this last night. Just don't laugh out loud in the dormitory. God knows you get enough of spiritual reading").

So tears melted into rueful smiles, anger exploded, fears vanished, and kisses brushed one's cheek. All that was demanded was silence in the conspiracy. Utterly true, we told no one — not even each other. We knew only that these moments of humanity, like touches of gentleness in a night of terror, made possible the terrible austerity of conventual life. The endless round of Spartan days with their spiritless tasks — malodorous toilet bowls to be scrubbed to sweetness, infirmary sheets to be washed and rewashed, spotless corridors to be scrupulously dusted morning after morning, silence to be kept for longer and longer hours — these seemed somehow bearable because at some unforeseen moment of each day, there would be a surreptitious interim of laughter and affection with Sister Angelice. If she could bend her will to live a life she had never wanted either, then certainly we could. For reasons beyond our ken, God in His eternal wisdom had hand selected each one of the forty-seven of us to do for Him a work that no other person could do. He wanted us to live a life devoted exclusively to His concerns, to strive for detachment from self, to form an attachment to Christ that would, after two more years of novitiate, make it possible for us to vow ourselves totally to Him in poverty, chastity, and obedience. At first for a year, then for five, then forever.

The finality of that "forever" sent premonitory chills through our hearts. Of course we'd be tempted to leave, to think that we didn't *really* have the call to this demanding life. But that would just be the voice of Satan. The very fact that we were *there* testified to the authenticity of God's call. Certainly we could all remember the moment — at a senior prom, in the back seat of a convertible, on the verge of a promised trip to Europe — when something made it all crumble to ashes and we seemed to sense some finer thing we were called to. It didn't matter that you despised this gloomy motherhouse with its miles of gleaming corridors. It didn't matter if in the bleakness of your starving youth you smothered sobs at night in the thin narrow pillow. In the morning you would again take your place with the others in the big airy postulate, folding your long cotton skirt about your knees and awaiting the swish of Sister Angelice's serge habit as she swept into the room to mesmerize you one step further into the desert of religious life.

You must *will* to follow Christ. (Her serious brown eyes held us.) When, some day in the future, you had succeeded in filling your heart with Him alone, then the happiness that would flood you would compensate for everything you had left for His sake. God would not be outdone in generosity. He would repay us a hundredfold. And His grace, as St. Augustine reminded us, would work its way in us, "in hard material and against the grain."

Meanwhile, you found yourself with the best companions you could want — bright, wholesome, generous American girls as alike as a row of cookies from the same cutter, all of them looking toward fields white with the harvest, eager to bear to a parched world the refreshing good news of the Gospel. These girls would be closer to you than your own blood sisters. Two years later on Profession day you would part from them with a wrench more agonizing than that dreadful tearing which had initially separated you from your home and family. So Sister Angelice promised her postulants as she schooled them in the Rule morning after morning, preparing them to receive the habit. On that fateful day, they would be transformed into novices. The shining caps of hair would at last be veiled. The little military capes would be replaced by long closed serge ones topped by high, stiff Roman collars — capes beneath which hands could be folded away and only serious young faces left to confront the dread Mistress of Novices who would replace Sister Angelice. And as always, she was right. The night they cut our hair the desolation of the postulants was complete — in part, over the mutilation involved; in part, over our leaving Sister Angelice.

At seven o'clock in the evening we entered the darkened chapel two by two. The privacy was total. Only those on ceremony could be present: the Postulant Mistress, her face unexpectedly grave; the expressionless Novice Mistress; old Sister Mary Realmo, representing the Community Council; and to assist each, a novice with eyes studiously averted. In the dim light of flickering vigil lamps at our Lady's shrine, I could make out the gleam of scissors, the large willow baskets lined with sheeting, the bent heads of the postulants as they buried their faces in cupped hands. If your hair was long enough, it hung in two thick braids to make the cutting easier. If short, it was pursued in a series of artless forays that left the victim skinned and somehow shamed looking. After the first few cuttings, I couldn't watch any more. The sound of snipping shears, the strangled sobs of a few less Spartan postulants seemed to signal the end of youth and laughter, the end of beauty, the yawning of the dungeon. Thus did one separate oneself from the love of things seen and give oneself utterly to the love of things unseen. I fingered my own cropped head and felt that there should have been a death bell tolling.

But bell or no, in the days that followed we began to die to our old selves and to put on the new. (Years later, a Vincentian priest told me, "That's when I sensed there was something rotten in Denmark. After all, it was the 'old man' who'd had the vocation!") The initial cleavage from the past deepened as we entered the novitiate. It was now that the door really swung closed on the world. In the ensuing year we would be canonically sealed off. There would be no visitors, no "secular studies," no leaving the cloister. This is the year of spiritual testing. And only the staunch survive it.

One by one we had lost our distinguishing characteristics: first our possessions (listed and stored against our possible later defection), then our privacy. We were issued institutional clothing, assigned numbers, told when to bathe, distributed to dormitories, instructed in the rules, and finally, on Reception morning, given new names. In many ways, this was the hardest deprivation. I could stand the heavy cotton stockings, the ugly underthings, the torturing head-dress. But my whole being resented being stripped of my name when the archbishop announced publicly, "Agnes Griffin, your name in religion will be Sister Mary Ignatia." Ig-na-tia! My outraged ear fastened on that hideous initial syllable and my soul wept for the ugliness of the sound. In a burst of detachment I had left the choice of name to the inspiration of the Holy Spirit. He was omniscient. He had to know how I hated the name Agnes. He knew I despised all hard *g*'s. Yet here He had scattered the lovely "Mauras" and "Joans" and "Carols" to each side of me, and saddled me with a corrupted form of Ignatius Loyola, the military founder of the Jesuits. In my mouth was the acrid taste of betrayal at a very high level.

The loss of one's name was enormously effective in eradicating from the postulants any last remnant of "singularity." Absolutely forbidden from the moment of our arrival was the mention of anything which might set us apart from our companions. We were not to discuss nationality, the social position of our families, our family incomes, levels of education, opportunities for travel, and the like. Entering the congregation was like undergoing a corporate rebirth from which everyone emerged really equal at a level of deadly sameness. No one went so far as to suggest that we think of ourselves as fragments of a universal mind. (Our spirituality was too coolly Thomistic for this.) But we were constantly reminded that we shared one life in God. Together with millions of baptized Christians, we formed the corporate mystical Body of Christ. We were temples of the indwelling of the Holy Spirit. Distinctions among us, therefore, would be incongruous, unthinkable. The eye did not think itself better than the foot. The possessor of a doctorate was certainly no more precious to the community than was the housekeeper. (There was a funny story going the rounds, nevertheless, about the superior who shouted to the lifeguard attempting to rescue two nuns spilled out of their canoe, "Save *that* one. She just got her Ph.D.!") While, in the sight of God, the analogy was certainly valid, its long-range earthly effect was to encourage among novices a regrettable anti-intellectuality.

Unremittingly they were reminded that it was better to practice than to be able to define compassion. That it was possible (and preferable) to do both, and that these acts might reinforce each other, was as far from the mind of our Novice Mistress as from that of St. Thomas à Kempis. If, during novice instructions, you felt inclined to remark that Plato had spoken of connatural knowledge, you swallowed the observation as prideful and tuned out for the rest of the hour. This too would pass. And once beyond the novitiate, one could begin thinking again.

As I look back now, I observe in myself and in my companions a noticeable regression during the postulancy. Day after day we were urged to work for humility, dependence, the simplicity of a child, to try to be to our superiors as "limpid water in a crystal vase." The result was often a kind of infantilism and a resurgence of childhood needs for reassurance, security, affection — rewards for being (as to my mounting annoyance Sister Angelice invariably termed us) good "children," striving for self-abnegation, discipline, self-surrender to God.

In the novitiate, however, like Victorian children thrust from the warmth of a tender family circle into the bleakness of a state orphanage, we grew up in a hurry. We put on the habit and stepped unawares into a life that was to prove radically alien to each of us. Whatever our feelings about the first six months, we found the transition from the honeymoon of the postulancy to the icy asceticism of the novitiate, to say the least, bracing.

With Sister Majella there were to be no moments of humanity. With Sister Majella there would be unswerving devotion to the Rule. There would be unquestioning obedience, continual denial of self, a ceaseless rooting out of one's faults, and an incessant training in the submission of the will. There would, in short, be the putting on of Christ with a vengeance.

Our Novice Mistress gave herself no quarter. She expected to give us none. She marched before her novices like a goose-stepping Prussian general. I had always the feeling that I ought to click heels, drop my broom, and salute smartly whenever she appeared. And appear she did, frequently, and always unexpectedly. From the start there was between us an unspoken contest of wills. She had, months earlier, forfeited my respect by tongue-lashing a novice in public over some trivial infraction of an order. She had not missed the shock and contempt in my face. And I entered the novitiate with a score to be settled.

Sister Majella was convinced that, no matter how perfect the novice, there was at her core a fatal flaw of character. She saw it as her task to evoke this demon — to set the stage, if need be, for the inevitable exorcism of our hubris. However polymorphous its form, she could discern it at a glance. A contraband apple bulging out a pocket; a whispered conversation at the door of the chapel; a sympathetic arm twined about a disconsolate novice shoulder — these were moments of epiphany which in a flash revealed a hapless novice to Sister Majella as the weak, self-deceiving, luxury-loving Sybarite she had all along known her to be. Saddened by our depravity, Sister Majella yet remained sternly hopeful. She might not have been able to define faculty psychology even to herself, but she was a fierce believer. One must *will*. One must *pray*. And all would be well. Indeed, all manner of things would be well. An inadvertent Calvinist in her view of human nature, she never went so far as to see in us Melville's "painted harlot," but she came unnervingly close!

To the last moment of my two years as her novice, I paid for the effrontery of my unvoiced criticism. When duties were assigned, I drew the antiquated bathrooms used by the professed nuns. When classes were posted, I found myself with an additional corridor to clean ("after all, she *has* her degree"). On innumerable occasions I was privately castigated for pride of demeanor and attachment to my Postulant Mistress. I would be publicly corrected for vanity in dress, lateness to prayers, and a "particular friendship" with my partner. So we fenced our way from month to month. In the end it was a draw. I could be humiliated, but I could not be leveled. In a way, I had Sister Majella to thank for my perseverence. I would not be *pushed* out — and certainly not by her! We parted finally, without regret on either side, and without a truce. Deep inside my independent soul, I knew that it didn't augur well. That was my fatal flaw. And I could only hope to hang on till Profession day would spring me.

Profession day, the day of my vows, the day I put aside the white veil of the novice and felt the black one being slipped onto my head while the archbishop waited to receive our vows. It was both a beginning and an end. The novitiate was over at last. Dragonish Sister Majella was behind me. The world was all before me. But a very different world from the one I had left thirty months before. In December of 1941 Pearl Harbor had catapulted the United States into the war. There was, of course, no TV, none of us had radios of our own, even newspapers rarely found their way into the convent recreation room. As a result, World War II was at a strange distance from the nuns at the academy where I was missioned. We prayed a lot longer, adding an endless Holy Hour every afternoon during which we said Pope Pius XII's prayer for peace. We ate a lot less and tried to master the intricacies of rationing. We sold war bonds. We shared letters from home with their accounts of fighting in the Aleutians and the Solomon Islands and their guarded references to boys we'd known ("Four F, thank God!" or safely home or missing in action). My freshmen worked at the USO in town, took over for mothers on the late shift at the defense factory, sang unremittingly of "the wild blue yonder." I knew very little more than they of the grim realities of it all.

Writing this as Vietnam is winding down, a war that, like many another nun, I have actively tried to impede, I find that earlier isolation from life almost unbelievable. It was an astonishing self-exile, a spiritual focusing of one's energies and sights as total in its way as the withdrawal of the Carmelite or the Trappist. *In* the world, we were effectively not *of* it. The system worked. There can be no doubt about it. And except for Selma, for Vatican II, for a handful of Franciscan nuns who mounted a picket line outside Loyola University in Chicago the summer of 1964, for me it might be working still. Instead, along with innumerable other American nuns, I have been almost totally assimilated into the contemporary world.

I look at my Mexican work shirt, and I think of the total lack of ceremony with which four years ago I took off the habit in which I had once been solemnly clothed. I find myself jammed into a film-showing with some two hundred black students down here at the bottom of the map in the Mississippi land-grant college where I teach. I think that I am here of my own choice, not under orders from a religious superior; that when I refuse to pay taxes to support a war I consider morally wrong, it is I who will tangle with the Internal Revenue Service. And if the path of my dissent leads to criminal proceedings, I'll have to take my chances, run my own risks. I have chosen to reinvolve myself in the world I once thought I had to leave in order to save.

The commitment endures, the essence of the life remains, though all the "accidents" of religious life have vanished like a dream. Not without a nostalgic backward glance, my congregation has resolutely moved into the modern world. The bright clouds of incense, the soaring Gregorian chant, the dark-veiled nuns in their medieval robes — with the rush into the future these have become the remembrance of things past. Their charm remains, their curiously evocative power of symbol, but they seem at once anachronistic and anomalous.

I have a new set of memories now, all of the recent past. There is the night we "kicked" the habit, the day we emerged upon an open-mouthed world in what we confidently termed modern dress. What had gone on behind the scenes was not to be believed. A score of nuns invaded the recreation room and eyed the ready-mades Sister Emily had had sent home for us.

— Let's see. I wore a twelve when I entered. But (despairing wail) that was twenty years and fifty pounds ago!

— God help us, Claire. You can't sit like that in a short skirt. They'll have the vice squad out.

— Well, that may be the way you wore your hair in 1942. But it makes you look like an elderly Shirley Temple now!

Someone gave us a shipment of bank uniforms — severely tailored bright blue gabardine. And for weeks we looked like a seedy branch of the First National. There were nuns determined to wear out any still serviceable convent item and who gave their smart double-knit suits the unexpected fillip of policeman's shoes. There were the reluctant sisters who clung to the veil, topping off a brown turtleneck sweater with a wisp of blue chiffon for a kind of Foreign Legion look which convulsed their students. Attendance records in our schools must have zoomed to an all-time high. For the first time in their lives, parochial school kids had a new occupational sport. They no longer had to guess whether or not Sister had hair ("I saw a nun in the hospital once, I tell you. It looked like there was an empty Sister hanging on the door and an old man in bed!") The new question was, "Is it a wig or isn't it?" As Sister moved from coif to coiffure only her superior knew. And, being in a similar situation, she was unlikely to talk.

There are, to be sure, moments of nostalgia: one searches for an earring and finds it tangled in a broken rosary. A snapshot forgotten in a book lent to a friend turns up on one's desk with a penciled "Wow!" on the back. Mother Teresa, the Yugoslavian missionary to the thrown-away poor of India, looks with luminous eyes out of a TV screen during the "Today Show" and one wishes for an instant for the veil which once symbolically bonded nuns. But that instant is fleeting. One knows that American nuns will never go back to an outworn symbol. Long ago, Christ suggested the essential sign that one was Christian — it had to do with loving one another. When we've managed that, it will be sign enough.

CHAPTER THREE

THE DRIVE TO QUESTION

The drive in us to move from standpoint to standpoint . . . I have called "the drive to question."
— MICHAEL NOVAK
Ascent of the Mountain, Flight of the Dove

How does change take place? Radical change in one's life? I *was* there. I *am* here. For thirty years I was locked into a system of my own choosing. Everything about my life was habit. Willingly I wore what Ambrose Bierce termed "the shackles of the free." Until the day when I realized with a pang that I no longer perceived these as freeing, but merely as shackles. That realization was long in the making, however. How does one unconsciously moment by moment untwist the strands of one's life until, as if on signal, they drop away totally?

It is 1970 and I am on leave from Mundelein College, Chicago, to teach at a land-grant state college in the South. Through a warm October night I lie unsleeping, mesmerized by the great orange globe that is the Mississippi moon. At a conscious level I untangle the bayings of the farm dogs across the field beneath my window. Deeper, I try to unsnarl the threads of experience over the past dozen years of my life. This is much harder. What was the first hint of change? The first premonitory cloud no larger than a man's hand idly observed along a quotidian horizon?

I think back ten years. Could it have been the summer of 1960 — my very first summer in Europe? Four heady months in England on a grant to research Charles Burney for a doctoral dissertation? (A trip, in retrospect, more exciting for days in the British Museum than for the mandatory pilgrimage to Lourdes.) Was it being loose in New York during the four previous years of graduate study? Years when, whatever the pressures, one never turned down a chance to catch Emlyn Williams on Broadway, Birgit Nilsson at the Metropolitan, Bernstein conducting at Carnegie Hall. One made new friends and met friends of friends, now and then glimpsing lives and worlds at an infinite remove from one's own.

The election of John F. Kennedy played its part, however minor. There was no missing the sense of pride and euphoria Catholics felt that January of 1961, seeing a Catholic entering the White House for the first time. At whatever distance, we all felt more directly involved in the political process somehow. Kennedy had got there partly by *our* vote. We had to admire the neat distinctions he made as he told Protestant ministers in Houston that he saw no contradiction between his Americanism and his Catholicism. He would not support federal aid for Catholic education.

And on Kennedy's heels came Pope John XXIII. With chagrin, I recall my initial disappointment when this rotund little man was elected to succeed the patrician Pius XII. From the outset, Pope John espoused, not international diplomacy in the style of his predecessor, but pastoral concern for his worldwide flock. It seemed an unpromising beginning. Why this almost unknown "interim" figure instead of the expected Montini? Within four short years, Pope John himself answered my question, emerging as a totally winning personality

— and an unpredictable one. He was to precipitate some of the most momentous changes since the Reformation and attract to himself the affectionate esteem of the entire world, Christian and non-Christian. In October of 1962, disregarding the dire "prophets of doom," Pope John presided at the dazzling opening session of Vatican II in Rome. Overnight it became the cynosure of the journalistic world. Yes, the ring of authenticity is here. With the Council, change perceptibly began.

Vatican II must really have been a publisher's dream. A spate of articles and best-selling books erupted from both Protestant and Catholic presses. Suddenly "spiritual reading" (our Rule required half an hour daily) took on a new luster. My tiny cell on the thirteenth floor of the College building became unofficial headquarters for lively early-morning rap sessions of a crowd of nuns bent on reading and discussing everything connected with the Council. What I remember now is not so much isolated ideas or insights as an eclectic blur of names: Oscar Cullman, Will Herberg, Schillebeekx, Danielou, Hans Küng, McAfee Brown. The Council was ecumenical and so was our reading — Protestant, Catholic, Jewish authors met and mingled as freely on the floor of my bedroom as at Jonah's Bar in the Vatican. Pretty heady stuff, we told each other, after all those years of *Fear Not, Little Flock* and *The Nun at her Priedieu*. Xavier Rynne's latest *New Yorker* letter from the Council passed from hand to eager hand as the rank and file discovered with delight that the hierarchy were perhaps the most political of them all. Almost audibly, the gates of our minds creaked open.

Simultaneously, it seems, a parade of visiting lecturers and scholars invaded the campus as Mundelein's president embarked on a one-woman crusade to update the religious community theologically. The theology department sponsored lectures by people like Bernard Cooke, David Stanley, Bernard Häring. R. A. F. McKenzie came from Canada, Harvey Cox from Havard. Rabbi Schalman invited Mundelein students to visit his Temple Emmanuel. Like a whirlwind out of Cuernavaca, Ivan Illich blew our minds for an exciting weekend. Cardinal Suenens came to Chicago to address six hundred mothers general and stayed at the college long enough to underscore the message of his phenomenally best-selling *The Nun in the World.*

The first American printing of that book was issued in 1963, the year that also launched *The Feminine Mystique.* At Mundelein both books happily made maximal impact on the faculty, for the College was at that moment launching a massive self-study directed by Norbert J. Hruby, who, had Betty Friedan not beaten him to the draw, would certainly have written the book himself. Instead, Hruby bought copies of Friedan, Carolyn Bird's *Born Female,* Simone de Beauvoir's *The Second Sex* by the half dozen, set up a tiny circulating library outside his office, and proceeded to confront every woman on the campus with questions about her identity, her promise, her shackles.

A massive questionnaire went to faculty, students, alumnae, even their husbands. "Some of the questions were downright unpleasant and some of the answers harrowing," Hruby admitted in the *Los Angeles Times.* Much of what we learned was predictable. Some of it was acutely uncomfortable. ("They said this was a dandy little old college for producing wives and mothers, but very second rate in creating intellectual interests.")* Translated, this meant that Mundelein was critically in need of women's liberation. Though this was a women's college, it was obviously not focused on their needs as persons. It was merely channeling young women into the expected slots and roles which awaited them in a male-dominated society.

* *Los Angeles Times,* February 26, 1966.

Amused, my secretary pointed to the irony of the fact that it was a group of women singularly free of male domination who were selling such notions. As if the nuns were in effect suggesting, "Do as we say, not as we do."

But were the nuns themselves all that free of sexist oppression? Hadn't the Vatican Council dramatized the fact that, when the chips were down, even the Church was an exclusively male preserve? In all that sea of Renaissance scarlet and lace — where was there a single woman? Only one of America's 180,000 nuns even made it to the Council and she only as an observer. Sister Luke Tobin, head of the Conference of Major Superiors of Women, got in, it was true, but she could not utter one word in that supposedly universal meeting of Christendom. I had to ask myself: were nuns truly out from under male domination?

Hruby set me thinking critically, not only about higher education in general, but about Catholic higher education, and specifically about women and how we educate them. He had established an advisory committee for the Self Study — Bernice Brown Cronkhite (dean emeritus of Radcliffe), Joseph Sittler (Lutheran theologian from Chicago U.), George Schuster (special assistant to Notre Dame's President Hesburgh), Professor Marston Morse of the Princeton Institute of Advanced Studies. Against the collective wit and wisdom of these distinguished people, our own ideas ricocheted. Virtually everything was brought into question, including Mundelein's own viability. "Does this college deserve to survive?" its president had asked, by no means rhetorically. Not unless we developed a new and radical stance toward women and their problems. Not unless we developed a curriculum and a philosophy which spoke to the contemporary needs of American women. I read Mary Ellman's *Thinking About Women* and found myself interpolating a mental "Yes! Yes!" page after page. To her, sex roles in our society were growing nearly superfluous, and the vaunted sexual uniquenesses quite obsolescent ("her" reproductive capacity; "his" physical strength). The image of the male mind, she claimed, was one that "breaks through"; that of the female, one that "broods."* How should young women be educated? The problem tantalized me. Was all this discussion on our part an exercise in futility? Once their sights were lifted, wouldn't women decide for themselves? I began to feel a responsibility to raise such questions for a wider audience.

College deans are naturals as luncheon speakers. So I stopped dodging half the invitations which crossed my desk, began shrewdly selecting my opportunities. When in September of 1965 the Archdiocesan Council of Catholic Women asked me to address the fifteen hundred delegates to its Biennial Conference at McCormick Place, I jumped at the chance. Since I was one of only three women on a long roster, I felt it my duty to appear. Then, the night before the meeting, I read the *Chicago Tribune* story on the conference. Not one woman speaker was mentioned. Into my wastebasket went "Higher Education." Into my Smith-Corona zipped a fresh sheet of paper. "Women of the world—" I began, and warmed to my subject as I talked about being "Born Female." I got a modest ovation on that speech. And I detected real passion in the response of my audience. It set the tone for a dozen later talks about women and second-class citizenship.

When NOW eventually hove into sight, I personally had long since been convinced that, after blacks, women are the largest underprivileged group in America. I had been struck by this fact when reading James Baldwin's *Nobody Knows My Name.* I could substitute the world *women* everywhere Baldwin wrote *Negro* and the context still ran true. I was beginning to realize that prejudice against

* Mary Ellman, *Thinking About Women* (New York: Harcourt Brace, 1970), p. 13.

37

women is ancient, ubiquitous, and deep, and will be monumentally hard to eradicate. Anthropologists, social psychologists, even theologians have exploded the cultural myths of female inferiority so entrenched in the popular imagination. But a staggering information gap separates the scholar from the person on the street. Even Pope John made no great impact on the Catholic mind when he described women as an emerging population. "It is obvious to everyone," he wrote in *Pacem in Terris*, "that women are now taking a place in public life . . . they will not tolerate being treated as mere material instruments, but demand rights befitting a human person both in domestic and public life."*

The more I read, the deeper my realization that American women had been sold a bill of goods, the more I came to see that it was not women alone whose rights were being overridden in our society. In terms of personal autonomy, in terms of power, women were without doubt a minority. But what of the racial minorities in America? What of their oppression? Just where did we stand — as Catholics, as nuns, as educators — on the question of civil rights?

A handful of Franciscan nuns unceremoniously forced that question one hot August day in 1964 by joining a group of demonstrators outside the Illinois Club for Catholic Women. When the Frank J. Lewis Foundation had given Lewis Towers to the university as a downtown center the club was permitted to retain its headquarters there and it had opened its swimming pool to Loyola students. Now a black university student had been refused admission to the pool. The dramatic result was nuns on a picket line. All of a sudden we found ourselves juggling a very hot potato.

That single outrageous act shook Chicago's Catholics and brought me personally up against the realization that I wasn't who I thought

* *Pacem in Terris*, I, Sec. 41.

I was. Or perhaps that scores of people took nuns for something that I did not. Trying to deal with the fact of those nuns on a picket line precipitated the rest of us into a major identity crisis. Deep within ourselves, beneath the surface serenity of our lives, we began probing for explanations. In some way all of us were implicated in that not-to-be-believed picket line.

I heard about it first from my sister Marion, who caught the news on TV and immediately marched to the telephone. "Who *are* those disgraceful nuns? Are they BVM's? I just hope the cardinal puts a stop to *that* performance." When I was able to put all the pieces together, "that performance" turned out to be the most unlikely in the world. It involved half a dozen nuns, graduate students in Loyola University's department of sociology. Wrapped in their brown habits, their veils flying incongruously about their staunchly held poles, the nuns made instant news. The *Tribune,* the *Sun Times,* the *Daily News* had photographers on the scene in moments. "Proper" Catholics were incensed by this public display. How could nuns so demean themselves? What kind of nuns would brazenly appear on a picket line? And in front of a Catholic institution at that? It was unheard of.

Long after Sister Angelica and her fellow pickets had vanished from public view, the debate raged on. Around scores of suburban dinner tables, within dozens of cloisters all over the country, activist nuns were suddenly the "in" topic. The college community at Mundelein split down the middle. On one side there was a good deal of long-upper-lip disapproval; on the other, expressions of delight that there were nuns with the courage to take a position on something besides the Legion of Decency. If you were "con," you talked about "unladylike, unrefined, vulgar display." You thought that the religious habit was disgraced, or you thought that there was something official looking about such actions, that they implicated everyone else who wore the habit but who didn't share at all the radical notions of the demonstrators. You wondered aloud with some asperity if these Sisters' superiors had given them "permission" to be on the streets like this.

If you were "pro," you found yourself defending the picketing nuns as truly radical in the root meaning of the word. That's what nuns were supposed to be, wasn't it — radical witnesses to Christianity? If *they* shouldn't take a public position, who should? And if the habit got in the way, well — what was the religious habit all about, anyway? Wasn't it supposed to symbolize poverty and Christian concern? Weren't the nuns who had picketed individuals even if they looked like every other nun in the order? They *were* persons, weren't they? They *did* have social consciences, didn't they? And, as Americans, they had a legal right to public protest. Moreover, what about the *issue* raised by the pickets? Wasn't the fact of racial discrimination more important than the picketing itself?

From the point of view of many Catholics, the answer to that final question was "Certainly not." Not if the pickets were nuns. It became increasingly clear that most Catholics thought that nuns were not citizens at all. Or if they were, not of this world in any event. They were on their way to becoming first-class citizens of Heaven and that should be enough for them. Let them stay off the streets in the City of Man.

At Mundelein this realization generated heated conversations which sprang up at dinner and spilled over into the recreation period. I stopped being bored and began showing up every night. Not infrequently the newly hatched radicals among us were still at it late the same night, debating the matter in impassioned whispers far beyond Solemn Silence. Now that I go back and try to piece it together, I see those midnight conversations as a turning point:

they launched us into a total reassessment of contemporary American life.

By the time the smoke of battle had cleared, and long after I had given up defending nuns with picket signs in snappy arguments with my sister Marion, I remember coming to the realization that lots of people (even people who loved us) didn't really know who nuns were. In films like *Come to the Stable* and *Lilies of the Field*, Hollywood had done its job well. Even our closest associates thought of us as quaint, innocent, otherworldly creatures swathed in miles of serge and yards of veiling. We were to be protected, even pampered, and certainly sheltered from such unseemly activity as promoting boycotts. Amid all the tumult and the shouting over marching nuns, very few seemed to remember who it was the nuns had set out to follow: a rabble-rouser from north of Galilee who wore sandals and a beard, drank wine with God knows who, and hung about the streets with known sinners. The nuns had taken vows to be poor (like Him), unmarried (like Him), and (like Him) strictly obedient to the law of love. Why then was everybody surprised to find them standing in the streets with the poor and dispossessed? Was it, we began to ask ourselves, because in actuality we were perhaps closer to the movies than to the Gospel?

Such an unnerving question led to some of the most intense self-examination American nuns have ever undergone. Over and over we asked ourselves:

— What does it mean to be a nun in twentieth-century America? If, as Harvey Cox was writing, Christians have to find Christ in the heart of the secular city; if being a Christian means being *present* as Christ was wherever there is alienation, injustice suffering, does it any longer make sense to leave the world in order to save it?

— What do the vows mean to us today? If our standard of living is typically middle class, can we really claim to be *poor?* Should we try to be? Does a vow of poverty commit us to a life of actual deprivation out of which we are unable to help others? Or does it commit the nun to a simple, detached life with a special responsibility to diminish the sum total of poverty in society by striking at its roots: ignorance, disease, exploitation, unjust economic structures? Cox was insisting that, instead of painting the peeling walls of some tenement kitchen, Christians should be dealing with urban problems at a sophisticated level inaccessible to the poor. Might this be the meaning of the vow of poverty in the modern world?

— What is the meaning of chastity today? Is it a sign of an exclusive love of Christ? Or is it a sign of an inclusive love for all men? Is it pragmatic rather than mystical? Is it meant to free us from the cares of one family so as to make us available to the most neglected in the wider human family — not only to the students in our Catholic schools, but to kids in the city public schools as well?

— What is obedience about now that we have a right to expect superiors to give us reasonable (or at least reasons for their) orders? Does it mean a deeper obedience to the law of Love, a responsible freedom to obey that law in the most creative and productive way we can?

These were the perplexing questions we asked ourselves in the months which followed, far oftener than we said among ourselves, "What shall we wear?" Though in the popular press that latter question became the most dramatic of all, by 1966 most of us were already convinced that old-fashioned floor-sweeping nineteenth-century habits had to go. Not because they were out of style. (Pauline Trigère correctly warned us that if we let long skirts go, fashion would snatch them up!) Not because they were empty of meaning. But because they were such powerful symbols. They connoted to

42

many people all that symbolized the pre-Council Church: authoritarianism, separatism, irrelevance, a ghetto mentality, flight from a world which might seduce one away from God. Vatican II said: Change all that. Embrace the world, all men, all faiths. Get involved in the solution to twentieth-century problems of war and poverty and overpopulation and the anxious fear that God is dead. We saw the Church attempting to renew itself, putting on new garments, fresh and contemporary, in order to speak to all men without artificial barriers. Either the American nun would do this also, or, prophesied Sister William, president of Immaculate Heart College, "She will quietly fade from the scene. She may say more but she will be heard less, unless and until she is willing to put her body where her words are."

When Selma came, I was one of many American nuns ready to do just that. On March 23, 1964, Martin Luther King went on national TV and urged every American outraged by events on that now infamous bridge to come to Alabama. The response was massive. Schooled by ten years of outrage against southern blacks, the American conscience stirred and wakened. The Little Rock school crisis, the lunch-counter sit-ins, the voter-registration drives, the freedom rides through Mississippi, the murders of Medgar Evers, Malcolm X, the civil rights worker in Philadelphia melded and peaked. The man from Birmingham Jail spoke with a kind of moral authority. There was no way to turn his plea aside.

At Mundelein twenty-seven students and eight faculty members climbed aboard a chartered bus and headed south. Half a dozen of the students were black; six of the faculty were nuns. The bus was stocked with sandwiches, canned juice, a thermos of coffee. People hauled aboard blankets and pillows and raincoats, "bedding down" for the long trip. It was dusk when the driver swung away from the campus, but a crowd of well-wishers swarmed around to see us off. For the moment gaiety flared. In the excitement of fare-wells and shouted injunctions, we forgot momentarily where we were heading. The set jaw of our uncommunicative driver re-minded us. I suspected that he'd just been routinely assigned to the trip. And he obviously didn't relish driving that busload of gung-ho liberals onto the unwelcoming terrain of Alabama.

Warned to avoid trouble, we made no stops along the way. If the black students couldn't stop for food, couldn't use the restrooms in the tiny Tennessee towns we skirted, none of us would. Next morn-ing, nearing Montgomery we caught our first glimpse of Alabama's red clay soil. We also had our first glimpse of grim-eyed troopers, their clubs at their sides, their faces hostile. It was deathly still aboard the bus now. The route had been carefully marked out for us: no one was to leave the bus till we reached the big sprawling campus of the City of St. Jude, a Catholic school where the marchers were assembling. Unbelieving, we stared out at the hate-filled silent faces which lined the narrow streets. To pull into the school grounds, to feel the rush of warm, damp air blowing in as the doors at last parted, to feel the welcoming arms of strangers lifting one down — it was coming into the Promised Land!

The school field was already densely packed. We found a vast assemblage of young and old, black and white, sprinkled with yarmulkas, miniskirts, Roman collars, blue jeans, trailing habits, budding beards, and "natural" hairdos. Except that every weary sweat-stained face seemed somehow radiant, it might have been the Last Judgment. Newcomers lined up outside instant johnnies, headed for coffee, got pulled into sobering self-defense sessions, found themselves clutching mimeographed diagrams of the march route as they swung into the endless line snaking its way out of the park. Somewhere Martin Luther King was winding up a sixty-mile hike from Selma. He would join our lines and we would all pour into the streets of Montgomery, heading for the square in front of the capitol where Wallace was expected to meet us.

We spread out across the pavement, our arms tightly twined about those of the marchers to each side of us, black-arm-banded marshals forming a wall of protection along the curbsides. Waves of song sporadically swept across the line, "Way Over Yonder," "Ain't Gonna Let George Wallace Turn Me Round," "We Shall Overcome."

At the end of the march, gulping down my allotted swallow of Coke from the bottle passed along the line, sitting in the streets forming bookends with a big, red-haired stranger who turned out to be a professor of classics at MIT, I had the deepest sense of community I have ever experienced. My shoes were broken and crusted with red mud, my habit was a shambles of dusty, rain-spotted serge, my veil was knotted under my chin for security. I was at the farthest remove from the crisp, immaculate Hollywood nun. And I was undeniably happy.

King had asked for a gigantic flooding of people into Alabama in a show of solidarity, a rejection of Bull Connor tactics for dealing with black Americans, an indication of American determination to confront racism in the South. We came to do these things, ashamed for the image of cruelty and injustice Alabama projected, convinced that in our own hearts there was no racism, that we were color-blind, as ready to accept the black as the white. Selma gave us a new perspective. We came back north, looked about us with new eyes, and recognized with shock the de facto segregation of our lives.

I had grown up in Chicago and taken it for granted that Negroes lived on the South Side. No one ever used the word ghetto. It was just where "they" lived. And there were none of "them" in our lives. In uptown Chicago where my father took us to live in the twenties, there was a single street we weren't to walk down — Clifton Avenue, where "they" lived. Occasionally we did it anyway, just for the thrill, just for a chance to dart a curious look at pink palms, narrow ankles, flaring nostrils, kinky black hair. It never occurred to me that none of "them" went to school at St. Thomas of Canterbury. I never missed "them" in high school or college. As a nun teaching in a Catholic college, I didn't think it strange that only a handful of black girls found their way to the North Side. I didn't puzzle over the fact that in a city with one of the largest Negro populations in the world, no black Chicagoan had ever entered our congregation. Like thousands of my counterparts in America, I was utterly purblind. To me these people had been invisible.

Now for the first time I saw with embarrassment how lily-white we were — our schools, our novitiate, our congregation. For the first time I realized how homogenous we were — white, mainly Irish Catholic, middle-class Americans who saw politics as a dirty business, voted a straight Democratic ticket, and aspired (by parish assignment) to the suburbs. King had had a hidden agenda in getting us Northerners south. And it had worked.

The night we got back from Alabama I had a chance to discuss our experiences on "Tieline," a CBS radio network program. It was news after all — a woman, a nun, a college dean. Eventually I found myself on another little lecture circuit, talking to parish groups, alumnae, women's clubs, Protestant church groups — explaining what nuns were up to, why we saw political and social involvement as part and parcel of being Christian. Why we felt ourselves guilty, part of the problem.

Suddenly, too, I found myself caught up in a rush of civil rights meetings. Dick Gregory, James Bevel, Al Raby stopped being names in the news and became people with a lot to tell us. We crowded into West Side churches to hear Bevel tell us how racist we were, how much we had to undo. We brought Dick Gregory to campus, entranced with his humor, sobered by his seriousness. We read our Baldwin, our Ellison, our Cleage, our LeRoi Jones. Nuns demonstrated in Gage Park and in Lawndale. Out in California they joined Cesar Chavez in protesting the conditions of the migrant workers in Delano. In the Midwest we began raising money for "Project Equality." The firing of a white BVM principal by a black pastor became a sign of contradiction and omission. It looked like a humiliating rejection when Father George Clement of St. Dorothy's parish school asked the nuns to leave. We BVM's had been proud of staying there in the "inner city." Now it was clear that we weren't wanted. To get out and to know why was the beginning of a practical understanding of the racial situation.

Painfully, we began to make distinctions between personal prejudice and institutional racism. The report of the Kerner Commission suggested that the authorities must bear much of the blame for violence in racial demonstrations. However we looked at the matter, we were clearly part of the Establishment, an Establishment we had not leavened with the principles of Christian dignity and justice. We had ridden through the night to Selma, indignant that southern police maintained order with electric cattle prods and fire hoses. And we had left behind us a house that needed badly to be put in order. If our parochial schools exhibited de facto segregation, if our college admission policies revealed implicit racial biases, if our employment practices exploited members of minority groups (think of the Catholic universities which used only black or Puerto Rican help in the kitchen), it was time to assess our own institutional racism. The walls around our tight little insular Catholic world were crumbling fast. Vietnam brought them down.

From the spring of 1965 right up to the Kissinger–Le Duc Tho negotiations for peace in December, 1972, Catholic voices had been raised in moral protest against United States involvement in the

Vietnamese war. The most famous "prisoners of peace" (as Phil Berrigan termed them) were, of course, the Berrigan brothers. A bizarre trial for conspiracy named a Roman Catholic nun among the Harrisburg defendants charged with a plot to abduct Kissinger and blow up the heating tunnels to government buildings. Sister McAlister was initially found guilty of smuggling letters into Lewisburg federal prison in reply to those Father Philip Berrigan smuggled out to her. In a countersuit she and a codefendant sued the FBI and the Justice Department for tapping their telephones in 1970 and 1971.

One had to admire these Christians who took seriously their roles as peacemakers. In his first encyclical letter, *Ad Petri Cathedram*, Pope John had reminded Christians of their moral obligation to strive for peace with every means at their disposal. Pope Paul pleaded before the United Nations, "No more war. War never again." In the Berrigans and their followers, the American public was privileged to observe fellow citizens who combined the best of American civil disobedience with the best of Christian obedience.

When in May, 1972, twelve New York Sisters of Charity, wearing white sheets that symbolized the dead in Indochina, lay down in the aisles of St. Patrick's Cathedral after Holy Communion, Cardinal Cook did not interfere. Seven of the nuns were arrested leaving the church, but the archdiocese would press no charges. This despite the fact that one of those arrested, Sister Patricia Harding, suggested to reporters that if he were really opposed to the war, Cardinal Cook would resign as military vicar to the armed forces.

By now, such protest drew little adverse notice in the Catholic press. Perhaps the Catholic public had grown inured to the sight of nuns demonstrating in the public sector. Certainly it had been otherwise in the early days of protest when it was difficult to involve anyone — let alone nuns — in public criticism of the war. I can't recall precisely when or how I was drawn into this kind of activity and became a sponsoring member of the Chicago branch of Clergy and Laity Concerned about Vietnam. What I saw on TV and what I read influenced me most, I think. The conflict was, of course, reported daily in hundreds of newspapers and journals. Some first-class journalists had undertaken lengthy treatments of the war that tried hard for objectivity, walking a fine line between the hawks and the doves in the news media. I was impressed and angered by Dorothy Dunbar Bromley's *Washington and Vietnam*, a concise analysis of the political and moral issues.*

Harrison Salisbury did a revealing series of articles for the *New York Times*, Arthur Schlesinger and John C. Bennett grew increasingly critical of American foreign policy.†

Then early in January, 1966, the Committee of Clergy Concerned brought to this country a leading South Vietnamese Buddhist monk, the poet Thich Nyat Hahn. I heard him speak at the University of Chicago and was deeply moved to hear a firsthand account of the war from the point of view of a distinguished, religiously committed man who was neither pro–Ky government nor pro–Viet Cong, but for the Vietnamese people, the peasants who had no voice. What Thich Nyat Hahn urged on Americans was essentially the same program which UN Secretary-General U Thant would call for the following June: (1) to cease at once the bombing of North Vietnam; (2) to begin a phased withdrawal of American troops; (3) to open negotiations at once including V.C. at the table; (4) to begin a massive rehabilitation program in Vietnam. Thich Nyat Hahn and U Thant addressed themselves fundamentally to questions of justice and peace

---

* Dorothy Dunbar Bromley, *Washington and Vietnam: An Examination of the Moral and Political Issues* (Dobbs Ferry, N.Y.: Oceana Pub., Inc., 1966).
† Arthur M. Schlesinger, Jr., *The Bitter Heritage: Vietnam and American Democracy 1941–1966* (Boston: Houghton Mifflin, 1967); John C. Bennett, *Foreign Policy in Christian Perspective* (New York: Scribner, 1966).

but they did not shrink from addressing the moral issues of that regrettable war. These disturbed me greatly. Whatever the causes of the war, whatever the legality of our presence there, I felt that I must in conscience protest the *way* in which Americans were fighting. I felt I had to play my part in raising the moral issue wherever and however I could.

On December 17, 1966, I had a chance to do this with maximum coverage by the news media when the Committee of Clergy Concerned joined with the Church Federation of Greater Chicago, the Chicago Board of Rabbis, and Mundelein College to sponsor a convocation on the "Ethical Implications of Vietnam." Despite city-wide publicity, only about a hundred people attended this meeting. But the *Chicago Daily News* that night ran a five-column story on the conference, including verbatim my criticism of our moral stance in Vietnam. The barrage of criticism I received (some from within the community), the scores of hate letters and telephone calls in the wake of that story, taught me firsthand how un-Christian Christians can be when incensed.

I had had a foretaste of public disapproval after appearing as one of four "New Nuns" on the "David Susskind Show" the previous March. But that had been mere mild knuckle-slapping for crossing my knees before the eyes of sixty million Americans. Obviously it was one thing to talk about religious life. To criticize the government for patent immorality was something else entirely.

Looking back now, I see how unfashionable it was thus to protest the war in 1966. The Catholic bishops (with the notable exception of Bishop James Shannon) were slow to take a position on the war. To my great regret, they did not participate in the mobilization sponsored by the National Committee of Clergy in Washington, January 31 to February 1, 1966. It was the ecumenical antiwar groups like Clergy and Laymen United Against the War which did provide a channel for a steadily growing stream of lay Catholics, nuns, and priests who, in accordance with *The Constitution on the Church in the Modern World,* exerted the pressure of a Christian conscience in public affairs.

In the summer of 1967, when I was seriously weighing an invitation to visit North Vietnam as a member of a four-woman peace team, Mother Consolatrice left the decision up to me, but admonished gently, "You will see Cardinal Cody — as a courtesy?" I was on the point of leaving for Miami to attend a meeting of the executive committee of the American Association for Higher Education and time was very short. Knowing it might take months to get an appointment through the normal channels, I wired the cardinal from Florida telling him my plans and asking for an immediate appointment.

Our meeting in his North State Parkway residence was a gracious one. He had just come back from Lucy Johnson's wedding in Washington and chatted first of that affair. Sitting in that heavy, wine-red Victorian sitting room with its ceiling frieze of ecclesiastical designs, it seemed incredible to me that I was actually describing to him the venture I had in mind. The journey had great symbolic meaning to me — as an American, as a woman, as a nun. I did not see how I could *not* go. Not with the deeply held convictions I had developed; not with the possibility of finally putting my body where my mouth was, so to speak. (Even the cardinal smiled faintly at that mixed metaphor.) But he came on strong. And he supported the war to the hilt. For him there was only one way to end this conflict — for the United States to move in with all the power it could command and liquidate every last Communist to ensure a permanent peace with justice.

The irony of his language escaped him utterly. He was kind to me; he was paternal; in an old-fashioned, slightly patronizing manner he was concerned for my welfare. And he was concerned for the Catholics he said were being persecuted in North Vietnam. He wanted, however, to look into the character of the group which was sponsoring this trip to Hanoi. He had ways. He had power. He would do it this moment. When we parted, it was with the assurance that I would have a full report before I actually committed myself to going. Actually, Fate, in the guise of a ruptured disc, landed me in St. Francis Hospital when I should have been flying to Asia. But I never heard from the cardinal again.

Immobilized in traction, you quickly learn the vagaries of life on the magic mountain. Who will come; who will not; how long you can endure; how long you must. And you discover too, if you are lucky, an escape hatch. You can still read. Flat on your back, you learn to hold a paperback for longer and longer periods. And when the book is absorbing, it mercifully blocks out the buzz and hum of conversation, the endless peremptory signal bells, the mindless laughter of daytime TV. Of all the books I voraciously consumed those weeks, two stand out like Alpine peaks. Erving Goffman's *Asylums* was one, H. Richard Niebuhr's *The Responsible Self* the other.

Reading *Asylums* was like seeing my life under a miscroscope. Along with orphanages, sanitaria, mental hospitals, penitentiaries, and army barracks, Goffman designates conventual life as a "total institution," an establishment symbolized by the barrier to social intercourse with the outside and to departure that is often built right into the physical plant, such as "locked doors, high walls, barbed wire, cliffs, water, forests, or moors."* Though they do not exhibit all these characteristics, such institutions do share at varying degrees of intensity a perceivable family of attributes. Goffman indicates his in-

---

* Erving Goffman, *Asylums* (New York: Doubleday, Inc., 1961), p. 4.

terest in total institutions as sociological phenomena but pointed out that there are other reasons for attending to these establishments. "In our society, they are the *forcing houses for changing persons;* each is a natural experiment on what can be done to the self."* The essays which followed this fascinating introduction proceeded to analyze first the "inmate" world, then the "staff" world, and finally relationships between the two. Here at last I found a way to come to grips with the tensions so many of us were feeling as we tried to be nuns *in* but not *of* the world. What we were reacting against were the elements of totalitarianism which effectively nullified our efforts to be persons. Goffman could not show us *how* to effect change, but he could tell us *why* it must be brought about. His book proved to be a vade mecum for all the days of quiet revolution that lay ahead.

Niebuhr's *Responsible Self* spoke to me not in sociological but in ethical terms. I had felt myself inexorably involved in questions of public policy. Though physically separated from the world, I could not cut myself off morally. There was no way in which the excesses of American warfare in Vietnam, the oppression of the world's poor, the exploitation of sexual or racial minorities could be shrugged off as someone else's responsibility. The *Minnesota Star* might challenge the right of any clergyman, in clerical garb or mufti, to take part in public protests.† Catholic diocesan newspapers might deplore the "unladylike" conduct of nuns who picketed and protested. Even CBS had been intimidated by the powerful opposition of the New York archdiocese to my appearing on TV in New York City. Though I objected that my right of free speech was being denied, the producer backed down when Msgr. Thomas McGovern, vicar for religious, refused his permission for my appearance. Still it seemed to me that the majority of the American public had come to recognize that

* *Ibid.,* p. 12·(italics added).
† January 30, 1966.

nuns and priests do have the right to speak and act as private citizens. To keep silent on public issues which one privately condemns is by implication to endorse them. If there were painful differences in opinion among Catholics, if there were risks of governmental recrimination against those who actively opposed the war, these were merely the inevitable hazards of reacting as a responsible human being. In Niebuhr's words, conscience is a "function of my existence as a social being."* I had grown up thinking of conscience as the rational intellect passing judgment on the morality of one's acts. And, like most Catholics, I took those acts to be private and personal. Niebuhr, however, stressed the social dimension of conscience. It was not enough to allow one's light to shine like "a good deed in a naughty world." One had to admit one's share in the naughtiness and try to eradicate it.

Largely as the direct result of the thinking of men like Dom Helder Camara, the realization that to be a Catholic is to have a social as well as a personal dimension is very much au courant among informed Catholics today. Yet it was one of the most freeing concepts I myself arrived at in the sixties. For nuns especially, conscience had for so long been a private matter. It had for so long been preoccupied with searching out infractions of precise and absolute laws of conduct. Once the Church had defined matters of morals in terms of precept and law. After Vatican II when this seemed no longer possible in any blanket way, Catholics found that trying to form their consciences on matters of human rights, population control, social justice, personal relationships, and worship often placed them at variance with official Catholic positions. The context of ethical decisions became less legalistic, more complex. The context of conscience now seemed one of concern, of response, of dialogical

* H. Richard Niebuhr, *The Responsible Self* (New York: Harper and Row, 1963), p. 75.

interaction with others. Niebuhr's definition of conscience assumed man to be this responding, responsible self. "Conscience," he wrote, "enables a man to reflect on his own deeds by viewing them with the eyes of others."*

The Responsible Self projected for me an image by which to comprehend myself as a social being and to shape my conduct in relation to the other. Niebuhr spoke of the ethic of responsibility: one which is concerned with the fitting action. It "fits into a total interaction as response and as an anticipation of further responses."† As a nun, I had thought myself wholly oriented to others. Events of the sixties had unsettled any such conviction. The decade swept us from standpoint to standpoint, swirling a current of dissent around questions of Catholic isolation, the oppression of women, the civil rights movement, the war in Vietnam, the brutalities of the 1968 convention in Chicago. To their dismay, many nuns had discovered that they were living largely outside the arena of human life, mired in self-concerns of the most irrelevant order. The need to change became an imperative.

We asked ourselves deliberate questions. When human beings are poor, are oppressed, are under aggression — how do we respond to their action upon us? How do we interpret what is going on and determine on the fitting action? Not merely by pursuing the ideal good we have established as our own; not merely by examining the existing laws under which we operate; but essentially by seeing ourselves in a dialogical relationship with all other selves, by listening in order to hear, by answering as a social being.

It was into this kind of dialectic that American nuns had been drawn in the tumultuous decade of the sixties. Their honest unstructured responses lifted many of them out of the tightly woven

* *Ibid.,* p. 76.
† *Ibid.,* p. 61.

system which was conventual life. Their face-to-face encounters with the poor, the blacks, the real dimensions of the Vietnamese war raised questions about the total fabric of their lives. It was not one of these things which precipitated change. It was not all of these things. It was not the sum of these things. It was more.

Vatican II seemed to many to have thrown open the window on a fresh vision of life. We had thought ourselves immersed in change-lessness like bees in amber. We came to realize that if there were any constant in contemporary life it was change itself. Once we had thought it our task to change the world. But the most radical change we had first to effect was much closer to home than that. We had to change ourselves. And to free ourselves as persons, we would first have to "detotalize" our own institutions. We would first have to humanize the convent.

CHAPTER FOUR

THE POLITICS
OF CHANGE

*We of the present generation will be the last ones
capable of perceiving the difference between the
old and the new. Shortly there will be millions of
Americans who will never have known the
difference.*
— MALACHI MARTIN

The voice of the superior was the voice of God. And each August
15, God spoke in awful tones announcing the names of new local
superiors elected to govern for the ensuing four years. How many a
sniff and how many sets of pursed lips among the Old-Timers when
that vital roster was scrutinized. "Humph — all her old cronies from
the Immaculata, I see."

"But why not?" asked the Innocent Young. "She can't be expected
to know everyone in the community, can she?"

A withering glance from the Old-Timers on that one. For there
was an "In" group. No question about it.

Years back Mother Josita had been principal of the once prestigious Immaculata High School in Chicago. As a result, the congregation was liberally sprinkled with superiors, principals, novice
mistresses, even provincials who had grown up in that somewhat
aristocratic house under her shrewd brown eye. What more natural

than that in half the high schools across the thirty-five dioceses BVM's taught in, girls wore the counterpart of Immaculata's archaic blue serge uniform, and seniors sang their disparate loyalties to Immaculata's version of Schubert's "Marche Militaire"? If not in fact, at least in rumor, the Immaculata begot Mundelein College and patterns were reduplicated. The "In" group expanded and the "Out" group seethed.

A similar sphere of influence encircled key schools and key administrators in Dubuque, and no doubt in Los Angeles, Memphis, and New York. But Chicago was a veritable BVM ghetto with seven hundred BVM's assigned there in the heyday of the congregation. It was somehow easier to see "politics" at work in Chicago where the Kelly-Nash machine was a household word. But came the revolution — in the guise of renewal and reform sparked by Vatican II — and BVM's democratized with a vengeance. The voice from the summit became the voice of consensus. And the Chicago grass roots finally had their day.

Seen in retrospect, pre–Vatican II modes of religious life seem incredibly remote from the seventies; for the fact is that American nuns lived their lives under social, economic, and theological conditions which simply no longer exist in our time. To try to understand how this quondam institution operated, we have to re-create a model of life under obedience to a superior. Theoretically, this closely resembled a hybrid family-military model. Our head was both Mother and General.

All authority flowed from the hierarchical peak through a system of higher and lower superiors who, backed by the Rule or Constitution of the order, effectively regulated every least detail of the lives of their "subjects." (The term still connotes the inescapable aroma of sovereignty which clung more perceptibly to some than to others in command roles.) For some in the ranks, the behavioral reality, however, involved a unique politics called "beating the system," so that one could never be quite certain whether one's attempts at "perfect" obedience didn't look to cynical observers uncomfortably like boot-licking.

The primordial elements of religious life involved the theologically grounded belief that God spoke directly to each Sister through her superior. Associated with this belief was a governmental structure giving the superior supreme authority in the domestic affairs of her own house, and making her the sole representative of her community to officials outside the house — the Mother General, the provincial, the pastor, the local physician, the janitor. This on a kind of "power speaks to power" principle so rigid that even the Rule warned, "Without the special permission of the superior, no Sister is allowed to invite anyone, even a relative, to a meal or lodging."*

My cheeks still burn when I recall the classic reprimand this community regulation once cost me at the hands of Mundelein's formidable Sister Mary Justitia. Newly professed, barely two years out of college, I was spending the day on campus looking up old friends. Since, according to Rule, a Sister was always to call on the superior first, I dutifully cooled my heels in her outer office for a full hour, feeling rather like Sam Johnson waiting on Lord Chesterfield. Finally, as my time dwindled, Sister Mary Anna Ruth bore me away to lunch. "Later" turned out to be three o'clock just as I was leaving to catch my train. Access to the Great Personage still being denied, I picked up the extension phone and got her at once. But my name had barely crossed my lips when the receiver crashed down in my outraged ear. Never one to lose face, I continued laughing and chatting away over the dead wire, assuring Sister Mary Justitia what a

---

* *Constitutions of the Sisters of Charity of the Blessed Virgin Mary* (Dubuque, Iowa: Mount Carmel, 1958), Chapter X, Sec. 148, p. 52.

pleasure it had been to visit my alma mater. And of course I'd be back again — very soon. How very gracious of her. It was months before Sister Mary Anna Ruth felt I could bear the truth. The switchboard had of course automatically signaled that I chattered to a dead end. Sister Mary Justitia had had the last laugh after all. For years afterward I never sat down as a guest in a BVM house without first having called on the superior. But I never forgot the singular rudeness of a women I had previously admired.

Local houses were grouped into one of four provinces, each under the authority of an appointed provincial answerable to the Mother General and her council, themselves elected for six-year terms by the General Chapter which met at stated intervals both for this task and to legislate other changes. Only in the election of delegates to the General Chapter did the rank and file have power to vote and then only under carefully specified conditions. No nominations were made, no campaigning was permitted, no discussion of candidates was allowed. The Spirit moves where it will. But chapter after chapter saw the return of veteran delegates, their number grudgingly augmented by an occasional younger superior. It was a supremely closed system. It was, ideologically, at the furthest remove from democracy.

Much of the effectiveness of the superior concept must be traced to a notion unique to religious. The "grace of office" this was termed — a kind of special protection or enabling grace extended by God to a superior to help her carry on her task, however inadequate to it she appeared in terms of natural endowment. In the light of this principle, superiors were, first of all, women of virtue, "community women" notable for their fidelity to the Rule, their capacity for hard work, their reputation for running a "tight ship." Only then, it seemed, did the council consider academic qualifications (superiors traditionally headed both convent and school), organizational abilities, facility in handling group relations and lay faculty members, and so on. Community lore was packed with legends about the tone-deaf Sister who was handed a violin and told, "Sissie, go teach the fiddle." Such myths survived because of their unmistakable ring of truth. Any summer school bevy of nuns could while away an evening's recreation with horror stories about superiors of similar ilk.

Yet in our more benign discussions we freely admitted that superiors were themselves victims of the system. It was hard for any superior to escape the assumption that she ruled by Divine Right, especially if a similar conviction led certain sycophants to cluster about her like courtiers flocking after the Sun King. In fact the whole enterprise seemed based upon the apotheosis of the superior as Supreme Monarch. Her function was to rule (benevolently, to be sure); the function of her subjects was cheerfully to obey to the letter. Simply that. With no opinions asked or offered. How else could one keep one's vow? Indeed, the ideal was prompt, total, and even blind obedience. "Insofar as an informed intellect can incline the devout will," Jesuit Father Wilson explained this concept in retreat, one great hand slowly forcing back its faintly resistant partner. Unless the matter of a command were manifestly sinful, the virtue of the vow specified generous compliance. Even if a superior's orders seemed stupid (watering a dry stick), one ought to obey. And spiritual reading was punctuated with legends about dry sticks which, being faithfully watered, had miraculously blossomed. Conventual climate was obviously not congenial to private initiative. It was, in fact, explicitly discouraged by Rule: ". . . they shall not introduce anything new, although this might seem to be better."* And it was laughingly agreed among the inmates that if one superior tore a wall down, the next inevitably put it back up.

* *Ibid.,* Sec. 51, p. 53.

The transformation of this highly structured, tightly regimented mode of life from a monarchical model to one of participatory democracy in the space of several short post-Vatican II years strikes even me as slightly less than miraculous. And in our congregation I happily had a hand in bringing it about.

Ultimately, the revolution in the Church goes back to John XXIII, elected to the papacy October 28, 1958. Early in 1959, he announced his intention to convoke the twenty-first ecumenical council at Rome, the first since 1870. And when the Council finally convened four years later, Pope John laid down its agenda: a renewal of the Church under the Holy Spirit, and a significant step toward Christian unity. Catholics everywhere, lay and religious, were to achieve an *aggiornamento,* an updating of themselves and their institutions in the spirit of the Gospel of Christ. Reform and renewal — these were keynote words, the open sesame to a new spring in the life of the Church. And the Spirit which moved John moved American nuns to an enthusiastic response. They who in many ways seemed most remote from the life of their times emerged as avant-garde agents of change not for themselves alone but for the various publics they reached, young and not-so-young, within and beyond the Church. The Conciliar principles of collegial authority, the primacy of person, the imperative of conscience, the universality of Divine truth suggested to religious men and women criteria by which to measure the essential Christianity of their own lives and institutions. The vast machinery of ecclesiastical change creaked into motion. The Council ordered all religious to prepare to hold special General Chapters which, functioning as mini-Councils, could officially legislate the changes needed to achieve renewal. By the time the Council ended with the closing of the fourth general session on December 8, 1965, the groundwork for unprecedented change had already been laid in most American congregations.

For us it all began with a three-week meeting held at Mundelein. The title came from one of John F. Kennedy's speeches and it couldn't have been more apt. The Institute on Problems that Unite Us led eventually to an extensive two-year Self Study in preparation for our Tenth General Chapter of 1967–1968. This was the Vatican-ordered "special" chapter which legitimized undreamed-of changes and altered the course of history for the congregation. Yet nothing of what it accomplished might have happened at all had it not been for that first totally unprecedented attempt to see where we stood in the summer of 1965 — to see whether we even deserved to survive if we could renew ourselves.

Mother Mary Consolatrice had the courage to convene the institute (self-scrutiny is always risky) and the genius to name as its executive director one of the most outspoken and perceptive members of her council. Sister Mary Frances Patricia is a woman of astringent bluntness offset by charm and a disarming wit. She set the tone of the institute by insisting that the 275 delegates include not only superiors but grass-roots members, not only BVM's but observers from other orders of women, not only nuns but Catholic and Protestant theologians, psychologists, philosophers, journalists. Michael Novak talked about poverty as "essentially . . . concern for the poor." Sister Mary Anne, BVM, warned against convent role-playing, "playing to the gallery, creating a self for others to know rather than being an authentic person." Joseph Sittler accused Church-related schools of failing to teach the most important thing, "the commitment to love." Jim O'Gara of *Commonweal* challenged nuns to break out of their parochial isolation and get on to the campuses of ivy league colleges and state universities where they could multiply their influence. Former Novice Mistress Sister Mary Leo flatly denied that one can grow in the absence of person-to-person relationships. "The more an individual Sister loses her self-preoccupation in the attempt to discover the inner person of another, the more she will mature, finding herself and Christ."*

Sister Frances Patricia prodded delegates to examine every aspect of their lives and commitments, pummeling them with question after question:

Is it worldly any longer to be eager to identify with the "secular city" in which we profess to be serving the People of God? Is it a betrayal of the Catholic school system to question its excellence; to seek perseveringly and creatively for a clear statement of philosophy that will make the system worthy to continue in existence; to lament the fact that we are unwittingly in our very own schools in *de facto* segregation? Is it a dangerous departure from tradition to agree . . . that what is called for is nothing less than a new vision of what God is doing in the world and of what the Church is called upon to do, together with the freedom to move out in bold experimentation to these new frontiers? Is it being radical to think that a dream too long deferred can only die? Is it being presumptuous to question the viability of an administrative structure that, because of the large numbers with which it deals, is unable to cultivate the uniqueness of each human person in the community? †

Gallons of coffee, a delicatessen of sandwiches, thousands of talk-hours later, when adjournment was the last item on the agenda, we shaped resolutions and adopted recommendations which dramatized the degree of change already effected in a group I'd found a good deal less conservative than I'd expected. On the practical level, we voted in a professionally run self-study. And we asked the Conference of Major Superiors of Women to demand that U.S. bishops appoint American nuns to the papal commission charged with revising the

---

* *The BVM Vista*, Vol. VIII, No. 4 (September, 1965), pp. 10, 8, 3, 4, 9.
† "Overview," *Proceedings of the Institute on Problems That Unite Us* (Dubuque, Iowa: Sisters of Charity, BVM, 1966), pp. xi–xii.

canons regulating the lives of religious women. (Wasn't collegiality about sharing in decisions affecting your own life?)

With an eye to action from our own higher superiors, we passed a series of resolutions. One asked for a two-year period of experimentation with all aspects of community life so that the chapter would have data from which to draw conclusions. Others urged superiors to encourage collegiality and subsidiarity (decision making at the local level) as well as responsible freedom on the part of the individual nuns. The final resolution showed that opening to the larger problems of society which Sister Frances Patricia had urged on us. It called for "the Congregation corporately and in its individual members to exert every effort to win for all men full human liberty, working actively through all possible channels to break down civil injustice and racial discrimination wherever these appear in American life."*

Our walls crumbled slowly, it is true. Though the Vietnam War had already escalated into a major conflict the preceding year, I recall little concern being voiced about American intervention in Asia. BVM's had marched in Alabama the spring before the institute. We'd come back self-consciously aware of what a blind spot most of us had regarding our own racism. There was some talk those three weeks about the right of nuns to picket, the need to separate out one's individual stance from one's community stance, problems that were surfacing vis-à-vis pastors and parents who wanted nuns behind walls, whatever Cardinal Suenens thought about their role in the modern world. But, as yet, our outlook was largely insular and Catholic with a large *C*. I remember arguing that nuns had a right as citizens to demonstrate politically. I also suggested that we experiment with a self-imposed night curfew on conversation

* *Ibid.*, p. 302.

instead of the customary bell for Solemn Silence. The latter suggestion drew fire and angry rejection. The former was still too remote
from the experience of most nuns to stir up any debate.

Undoubtedly the major outcome of the institute was the Self
Study. Mother Consolatrice named as director Father John V.
Marschall, a professor of history at Loyola University and a man
without ties to the congregation. Assisting him as consultants were
Dr. Bernard Hall, Menninger Foundation psychiatrist; Msgr. John
Tracy Ellis, historian of the Catholic Church; Philip Scharper of
Sheed and Ward; Sister Marie Augusta Neal, sociologist; Robert
McAfee Brown, Protestant theologian on the faculty of Stanford.
BVM's headed up the six major committees concerned with various
facets of community life and had on call two hundred and twenty-
five elected task-force members charged with carrying on the study.
Discussion meetings saturated the congregation and threw up some
twenty-four thousand questions which, edited into basic-issue statements, eventually confronted every member with the inevitable questionnaire. In April, five hundred BVM's met at the Claremont Hotel
in Oakland, California, to hear at first hand the reports of task-force
chairmen and to dialogue with the consultants as to what these first
tentative findings suggested.

Immobilized by traction in Chicago, I followed the news of the
Task Force on Government from St. Francis. This was my committee and it galled me to be out of action. Word filtered back.
Gossip surfaced. Reports were circulated. The real problems began
to emerge: community was obviously a major one. People admitted
to feeling that they were in effect living separate lives in the context
of an institution. Canon law prescribes "common life" (giving everything to the congregation and receiving all one's needs from it),
and most of us were living just this way. But in practice common
life seemed legalistic, juridicial, cold, impersonal. Instead of worry-

ing about "community" (the warm and human sharing of members with each other), superiors tended to worry about "common life," about how much financial leeway they could give the individual Sister. And she, in turn, anguished about how she was using "supply money" (petty cash on hand in one's classroom). What people complained about — hesitantly at first, openly later — was the loneliness of life in the congregation, especially in large houses where there was a conspicuous isolation, a conspicuous attempt to substitute organized joy for genuine friendship and open exchange.

Loneliness in community may have come as a surprise to many, at least to nuns who had spent most of their time on small missions of four or five, for they tended to envy those of us assigned to "big" houses. They probably thought we had choices and weren't confined to the same dreary round of chatter, the same unresponsive faces across the dinner table.

They forgot that people tend to cluster into congenial groups and that a large house of sixty breaks down into neighborhoods just the way any small city does. At recreation one found the bridge groups, the Chinese checkers buffs, the knitters, the news hounds, the loners. No matter that the conversation swirled around them, no matter that the Fannie May's stopped faithfully at their elbows, they lived at the fringes of whatever group was near. Charity dictated that one "offer up" an occasional evening with the local Ancient Mariner and generously include the Permanent Dummy in a round of bridge. But even as one did so, one felt certain that Christian charity showed for the chill thing it was. Genuine liking wears quite a different face.

Aware that isolation is endemic to large groups, superiors conscientiously sponsored group activities to "bring the community together." Fresh from the novitiate, I spent two carefree years at tiny St. Joseph Academy in Dubuque where recreation was a casual unplanned affair, with one or two tables of bridge and a handful of Scrabble aficionados. Transferred to Clarke College, I found myself in a community of some seventy nuns. But, mercifully, I was almost at once swept into the life of a resident-student adviser and rarely wound up at community recreation. Then, in 1954, I was assigned to Mundelein's English department and discovered to my horror that here there was no way out. This was a commuting school. And, except for a rare "free" evening, one was expected to put in an appearance at recreation seven nights out of seven. If you fell in with congenial spirits, the time flew. If you fell in with the pursed-lip crowd, you were in for sixty minutes of pure unadulterated torture.

In winter, one got away with this scant hour demanded by Rule. But in fine weather, things could go badly indeed — for there was a Mundelein myth that the Sisters loved outdoor suppers on the eleventh floor porch overlooking Lake Michigan. Let a gloriously balmy Sunday come along and the inevitable sign would appear on the bulletin board: "Supper on eleven; volunteers needed." If you were among the younger nuns (and I was), you signed up to tote chairs, to lug tables, to haul food from the ground floor to the eleventh via the one miniscule Otis cage reserved for the upper floors. From that point on, the day was lost. After supper people were certain to linger, watching the sails along the horizon, meandering from topic to topic in an effort to stretch out the conversation to as decent a length as one could before regretfully breaking away "to a turn at the switchboard," "to telephone," to find a book one absolutely had to have that very moment. (Once I manufactured a nonexistent caller only to be discovered within minutes ensconced on my bed with a novel!) Yet at evening's end everything that had come *up* had to go *down.* (And if you were young, as I was . . .)

When nuns complained of living in "an atmosphere of restrained courtesy," I knew precisely what they meant. They meant the pained look of forced companionship, the barely murmured word at meeting, the studiously averted gaze of those thankful for the rule of silence. Nothing can be chillier than loveless togetherness.

Were it not for a circle of mad friends — some eight of us who managed to inject a good deal of laughter and an occasional clandestine Schlitz into the routine — I too would have suffered from a "crisis in community." Among all the problems that filtered back from that California meeting, this seemed the most acute. One could deal with tyrannical superiors (eventually we just got rid of the very category). One could arbitrate with obdurate pastors and bishops. The general treasury could supplement an anemic bank account. Even the matter of habit could be dealt with experimentally. But community? Clearly some way had to be found to liberate persons from total institutions. If the Self Study turned up nothing more than that need, it would be wholly justified.

Eventually, of course, the study isolated other trouble spots — matters of personal growth, choice of work, the routine of prayer, modes of formation and government, all of which demanded serious and creative solutions. In November, 1967, another plenary meeting was held, this time in Chicago's Pick-Congress Hotel with thirteen hundred BVM's in attendance. Three things about that session come at once to mind. It was the first time most of us had seen each other out of habit (we'd made the break in 1966) and we cased hemlines like frenzied fashion editors at a Paris showing. And it was the first time that anyone had ever publicly suggested that perhaps the congregation just might not survive at all. "She makes me feel," confided the nun beside me, "as if I'm polishing up the brass on the Titanic!" "She" was Sister Dorothy Franklin, a well-liked, extremely forthright, and, ordinarily, very funny woman. But when she took the microphone in the Pick-Congress ballroom, she was deadly serious. We might solve all our internal problems,

Dorothy suggested, but if we failed to come to grips with the larger problems of the world "out there," it was doubtful if we were relevant enough to deserve to survive. Knowingly or not, Dorothy Franklin echoed Harvey Cox, who was writing that world renewal, not Church renewal, was the real goal. On the brink of the Tenth General Chapter (it would convene a few days later at Mount Carmel in Dubuque), her words had a prophetic ring. This chapter would prove to be the most crucial ever held by BVM's.

The Pick-Congress meeting also marked the first public suggestion that the forthcoming chapter ought to be an open one, with well-publicized agendas, opportunities for lobbying, and total news coverage to keep BVM's across the nation in living contact with this meeting which could radically change their lives. Later Mary De Cock (formerly Sister Mary Donatus) made the suggestion, speaking in the cheerfully disarming fashion with which she tends to drop bombshells. Black-eyed, apple-cheeked, a doctoral student at the University of Chicago Divinity School, she spoke with the authority of expertise and the quiet confidence of one accustomed to acceptance. She had chaired the Self Study Subcommittee on Communications which had plugged the Pick-Congress meetings into electronic media and engineered a 16mm film made on the spot. Now the same committee had come up with a design for an "open chapter." They recommended closed-circuit TV reporting of the event, daily news releases, the taping of plenary sessions, comprehensive print-photo-TV coverage for the general public.

People were aware that the talented, hard-working communications committee deserved major credit for the unexpectedly high morale which accompanied the Self Study. But there was great hesitation about invading the sacred secrecy of a canonical chapter. Traditionally, chapter sessions were as closed as the Curia before Pope John. Delegates were, in fact, sworn to secrecy. All that was communicated to the Sisters at the close of the General Chapter were the names of new officers and a set of Chapter Directives. Had there been sharp disagreements, close races, minority reports — these died in the prudent memories of the delegates. The congregation-at-large was shown only a united front.

The carefully honed report of the communications committee diagnosed what it saw as the greatest barrier to intracommunity communication, namely, "the attitude of secrecy which is part and parcel of the authoritarian and paternalistic type of government traditionally characteristic of the Church and religious congregations." Far from being a virtue, secrecy by those in authority seemed to imply that "non-official opinions are not worth soliciting, or that the 'rank and file' are incapable of understanding the problems that confront superiors." Dramatically foreshadowing Watergate, the report concluded: "Today when all world authorities are subject to a public scrutiny unequalled in history, secrecy in actions and deliberations makes the most respected authority suspect and the highest integrity dubious. Secrecy is the very antithesis of communication, and communication is the basis of trust."* The spontaneous applause which affirmed this proposition indicated that the "rank and file" were voting with the palms of their hands in favor of an open chapter. Now it was up to the delegates to act.

As the Chicago meeting broke up that cold November afternoon, I headed for the lobby to wait for a ride north and found myself on the edge of a little clump of chapter delegates I would soon be referring to as "Old Guard." All were veterans of the last several chapters. I was too politically naïve to read their abrupt silence for what it was — an early strategy session to beat the open chapter proposal. Some weeks later, however, an hour into the first debate of

---

* *Self Study for Renewal . . . Final Reports*, ed. Sister Rita Mary Benz and Sister Rosemary Sage (Dubuque, Iowa: Communications Center, 1968), p. 193.

the chapter, I would recall that impromptu caucus and realize what it had been.

Actually, the decision to open the chapter plenary sessions to all BVM's passed rather handily. The real fight came over enlarging the membership of the chapter itself. Aware that chapters of women religious tended to be somewhat elitist, the Vatican Council, in calling the special chapters, had given them freedom to increase their numbers beyond what the Rule prescribed. The young contingent (those under temporary vows) lost no time in selecting two representatives they wanted to add: one an instructor in philosophy (Dolores Dooley), one a budding theologian (Mary Donahey). The chapter elected them without demur but with the significant limitation that, not having made final vows, they could not by Rule vote for the election of the new general.

Next we elected as chapter members the four chairmen of the Self Study commissions. They had been chosen in community-wide popular elections and it could therefore be assumed that they would be acceptable to the congregation. Since they had not been selected as official electors, they also were denied voting rights. Blanketing in the Self Study commission chairmen in this manner excluded only one likely candidate — Mary De Cock, chairman of the ad hoc Subcommittee on Communications and the articulate spokesman for an open chapter. Over the question of whether or not to seat her as the last additional delegate, the chapter split wide open. Because of her singular lucidity, forthrightness, and political savvy, the "pros" wanted her in. For identical reasons, plus the fact that they sensed in her a lack of affinity for positions and candidates they endorsed, the "cons" wanted her out. In the end, after prolonged and frequently uncomfortable debate, Mary De Cock squeaked through with nonvoting-status. But the victory was a Pyrrhic one at best, for the fight over this issue effectively polarized the chapter at the very outset.

What we had hoped to avoid had occurred before we even got a look at the agenda for change. The "Traditionalists" and the "Modernists," the "Liberals" and the "Conservatives" had surfaced and been indelibly branded.

Sisters who had traveled from Memphis and Phoenix and Portland thronged the general sessions, crowded around closed-circuit TV monitors, avidly snatched up the newsletters. Personalities emerged and clashed (I had a running feud with my own Sam Ervin) in the healthiest free-for-all any of us had ever seen in the congregation. As election day approached, a slate of nominees was chosen; open hearings with candidates were scheduled; delegates were courted. A harrowingly close vote (22 to 21 on the fifth ballot) made Sister Roberta Kuhn the first president of the congregation and gave her two VP's with a mandate to function as a team. When the session adjourned on December 23, it was with the realization that, though the Traditionalists had carried the day with the president ("We must preserve continuity"), the Modernists were represented by two vice-presidents ("We must guarantee change") and the delegates still had a chance to shape the new constitution in the second session of the chapter. The structure of the new government, they were determined, would relocate decision-making power in the hands of the congregation.

The six-month interval between sessions functioned as a much needed buffer zone. When delegates reconvened the following June in Wright Hall's air-conditioned chapel, the psychological atmosphere had cooled as well. Perhaps because the tension of pre-election days had evaporated; perhaps because of the presence among us of a score of professional consultants and experts (we had our resident canon lawyer, Paul Boyle, for the whole summer); perhaps just because we had leisure enough to discover that all of us were complex and lined up on different sides of lots of issues, the polarities in the group dissolved. Delegates siphoned themselves off into their working commissions and closed in on the major tasks yet to be done. What went on in the commissions (Nature of Religious Life; Organizational Patterns and Practices; Personal Development in Community; Resources of the Congregation; The Congregation and the World) was the real work of the chapter. It was there that we hammered out the new life-style, the new job orientation, the new world perspective, the new vision of life in community; the new modes of government which were to characterize us as a post–Vatican II congregation.

Out of the welter of words which flowed from the commissions, a few living phrases suggest what were the vital centers of change. We spoke of *community,* not of common life; of *persons,* not of subjects; of *community representatives,* not of superiors; of *collegiality,* not of blind obedience; of *simple living,* not of poverty; of *friends,* not of fellow religious; of *promises not to marry,* not of chastity; of the *People of God,* not of the Church. We were, as a graduate student of sociology put it in his own glazed jargon, "debureaucratized," "detotalized," "democratized." And I, for one, was totally delighted with the whole metamorphosis. BVM life would in the future be different. It would be freer. It would be more real (as we all discovered when we had to pay the rent!). It would be richer because more relevant. It would be more human. So it would be more Christian. And certainly it would be riskier. One thing was certain: it would never stop changing. Perhaps the most permanent feature the chapter had built into the congregation was the possibility of continuous evolution.

In all this shifting landscape, one looks for the point of permanence, for the center which must hold when everything seems to fly apart. I find it, I think, in the concept of person which emerged during the chapter. It had surfaced first several years earlier in Sister

Mary Anne's institute paper which stressed the existential insight that one is born human, and *becomes* a person through relations with others. "To be means to be open to the other so that the person becomes himself in relation to the other. This is the basis for the philosophy of community, since as soon as we have persons-in-relation we are really talking about community."* The Self Study continued its examination of person, linking the notion to freedom and conscience. "The individual's concept of person will determine her interior freedom. The collective concept of person determines the freedom possible to the person within the community."† The Chapter Commission on Personal Development in Community expressed its collective wisdom on the matter in a paper significantly titled "Person, Freedom and Responsibility." Taking its cue from *Siddhartha,* its author conceded that "the knowledge of what constitutes person can be communicated. [But] the reality of living personhood is . . . a form of wisdom" which can be caught only from the authentic person himself. The paper developed key concepts at the heart of personalism — man's responsibility to shape his own destiny: his inability to subsist as "an enclosed block of reality"; his need for relationship, availability, and presence; love and freedom as sine qua non of personal growth.‡ Both this paper itself and the spontaneous observations in a similar vein by Sister Dolores Dooley, its author, made a deep impression on chapter delegates and on observers.

In the Committee on Government we made the preeminence of person a central pillar of our political rationale. Sister Ethel Dignan, clinical psychologist, outlined in the clearest terms the psychological

---

* "Changes in Approach to Person," *Proceedings,* p. 59.
† "Report of the Commission on Personal Growth and Development," *Self Study for Renewal,* p. 19.
‡ *Kinetics for Renewal,* ed. Sister Rita Benz and Sister Rosemary Sage (Dubuque, Iowa: Communication Center, 1969), pp. 105, 107, 108–110.

dimensions of personhood. And, speaking for the Commission on Religious Life, Sister Carol Frances threw the weight of her reputation behind the theological validation she developed. The primacy of person she described as sound Biblical theology: before Yaweh, the Sons of God are free and human, serving the Lord. And this reinforcement, more than all else, legitimized change for chapter members not wholly convinced by philosophical argument.

So the blueprint for change was drawn. Bypassing the old military-family model, we had, in effect, designed a whole new congregation. The center of power had shifted to the senate; the Mother General had been replaced by a president working in tandem with two elected assistants. Provincials, superiors — not only the authoritative titles but the very realities themselves — had been replaced. Divided into nine new geographic regions, the nuns would in future elect their own regional directors. Dispensing with local superiors, they would forge their own group decisions. Utilizing the new personnel board, they could compete for available jobs anywhere in the congregation.

The new governmental structures had not sprung full-panoplied from the brow of Jove. They had been hammered out on the anvil of grueling committee work by chapter delegates deeply persuaded of the centrality of person in community. The thrust was consciously toward humanization, toward justice, toward social concern. And, as the chapter ended, the way was opened for creative grass-roots experimentation in the direction of new life-styles. "Keep radical and keep moving," advised Robert McAfee Brown. On the heels of the Tenth General Chapter, this was literally just what BVM's did. Apartments were found, houses were rented, groups were formed. And, exhilarated by the novelty of it all, we launched a Walden experiment of our own.

CHAPTER FIVE

UNBELLING THE CAT

*They are required to be a standing example of all
the virtues. Above all they are called upon to
display serenity: the world asserts that they possess
it, and this assertion allows the world to ignore
their unhappiness.*

— SIMONE DE BEAUVOIR
The Coming of Age

In *Sartor Resartus* Thomas Carlyle pierces to its heart man's dependence on clothes. The man does not live, he suggests, who can "figure a naked Duke in Windlestraw addressing a naked House of Lords. Imagination, choked as in mephitic air, recoils on itself and will not forward with the picture. The Woolsack, the Ministerial, the Opposition Benches — *infandum! infandum!*"* One must agree with Teufelsdröckh. The thing's impossible. More's the pity, but clothes do make the man.

It was certainly naughty of me to consider it. But more than once, trapped in an auditorium or cathedral or chapter room crammed with nuns, I was tempted to a modified version of this exercise. Sans veil, sans cloak, sans gloves, cape, cincture, yard-long rosary, thrice-starched hood, fluted wimple — even the most awesome of novice

* Thomas Carlyle, *Sartor Resartus* (London, Paris, New York: Cassell and Co. Ltd., 1908), p. 53.

mistresses lost her power to intimidate. There is something about a defenseless double chin.

Catherine of Siena likened the religious habit to a portable cloister. One walked about the world, as it were, in a cell of one's own. However far from her monastery, the nun was still effectively cut off from the hoi polloi, set apart as consecrated, holy, literally untouchable. And in a world which once respected the inviolability of Christian sanctuary, the habit was indeed a protection. "God's Geese," as the French Daughters of Charity were endearingly termed for their beautiful white-winged headdress, could walk unscathed through the toughest of Parisian back streets.

By the late 1960's, American nuns were, however, seriously questioning the desirability of this self-separation. Granted that the habit powerfully symbolized one's dedication to spiritual values. Wasn't it possible that the symbol operated in two directions? I had been spat at on Forty-seventh Street in New York, chased off a Chicago bus by a virago brandishing an umbrella, and drunkenly entreated to "shay a Mash for me, Shister" by a parochial school alumnus deep in his cups. Obviously not everyone was turned on by the habit, despite the endless train and airport confessional stories every nun could muster up. The habit was admittedly a living symbol of changelessness in a changing world. Even aesthetically, something would be lost if it went. But it was also a signal of withdrawal. And the fact that our isolation was voluntary did not nullify the effects of our ghettoization.

Nuns were anonymous (they were everyone's "Sister"). Like Ellison's *Invisible Man,* they were even faceless. Not only did they "all look alike" when met in a group, most were forbidden by custom even to be photographed. Getting a snapshot of Sister at the eighth-grade picnic was the acme of adolescent daring. Only the discovery of Sister's "real name" outranked it. Clothing the nun in the habit of religion, changing her name when she took her vows — both were intended to change her identity, to launch her into a New Life in Christ. The result was what Erik Erikson, speaking of the Negro, terms a "surrendered identity." It hadn't been lost; but it had been repressed.

Moving into modern dress had dramatic impact. It revealed to the world in general the human being underneath the habit. But, more important, it revealed the nun to herself: it was an experience in recognition. The habit had emphasized the communal aspect of her life. Selecting her own clothes suddenly underscored the individual. Though the term may seem too large for the situation, taking off the habit created within religious congregations a true revolution of awareness. The power to choose is crucial to a sense of personhood. Trivial as the choice of one's wardrobe seemed to outsiders (perhaps only prisoners and the military can appreciate the delicious luxury of getting into mufti), it was a significant step toward the liberation of American nuns. It cracked the ancient stereotypes.

Simone de Beauvoir says of the aging, "They are required to be a standing example of all the virtues. Above all they are called upon to display serenity: the world asserts that they possess it, and this assertion allows the world to ignore their unhappiness."* How easily one can substitute "nuns" in this chilling description of unfreedom — for these women have indeed been the very archetype of imperturbable calm. As she takes the veil, Gerard Manley Hopkins has the novice ask to be

> *Where no storms come,*
> *Where the green swell is in the havens dumb,*
> *And out of the swing of the sea.*

* Simone de Beauvoir, *The Coming of Age* (New York: Putnam, 1972), pp. 3–4.

Even as the *Deutschland* founders and sinks in icy northern waters, amid the screams of the dying a nun serenely calls

> *"O Christ, Christ, come quickly":*
> *The cross to her she calls Christ to her, christens her wild-worst*
> *Best.*

To the poet she is a "lioness," a "prophetess," "The Simon Peter of a Soul!" And he asks:

> *Jesu, heart's light,*
> *Jesu, maid's son,*
> *What was the feast followed the night*
> *Thou hadst glory of this nun?**

It is doubtful that the unspoken expectations of Catholics regarding nuns have ever been expressed with more exquisite accuracy. Though not yet living perfect lives, they were described in pre-Conciliar language as existing in a "state of perfection." Religious life was a *higher* life. Its virtues were more than human. So deeply internalized was this goal of perfection that the nuns themselves spoke of chastity as the "angelic" virtue. Their prototype was Mary, the virginal, immaculate Bride-Mother of the Divinity. The explicit goal of the nun was to live every moment in the presence of God — to pray always, to keep her thoughts above.

In aid of this injunction, the religious habit served as continuous symbolic reinforcement. For the clothing of virgins the medieval Church developed some of its most beautiful liturgy and ritual. The veil covered the hair to indicate that the nun was espoused to

* "Heaven Haven" and "The Wreck of the Deutschland," in *Poems of Gerard Manley Hopkins* (New York: Oxford University Press, 1948), pp. 40, 63, 65.

Christ. The crucifix was worn at the side, a constant reminder of the redemptive suffering of Christ. The cloak covered the body like the renewing grace of Baptism. Black signified the nun's death to the world: henceforth she would live only to Christ.

One has to have stood before the bishop and received at his hands the consecrated habit of religion to understand the profound and ineradicable imprint of this clothing ceremony. The night before her Reception into the Religious of the Sacred Heart, Janet Erskine Stuart wrote of the incredible pain of knowing that never again would she ride across a field, never feel the wind blow through her hair.

To this high-spirited young nineteenth-century Englishwoman, taking the habit meant dying to the life she knew — English country life at its most comfortable, affluent peak. It cost her something to exchange a riding crop for a rosary. But no more than it cost her American counterpart symbolically rejecting the ancient family Ford if nothing else! For the habit severely limited personal freedom.

According to the BVM Rule, nuns could remove no part of the habit while in public. Since you seldom got to your room until after night prayers, this meant just about never. In our cells, we could (and most of the young ones did) take off the stiff veil and wear a filmy "soft" one. One might even remove the cape with its formidable two-inch stiff collar. But since one's bell might ring at any moment, summoning one to "the parlor," it was unwise, even had it been permissible, to go further. It speaks for itself to say that nuns had nothing to relax in. When the temperature soared to a soggy 110° in Dubuque, Iowa, summer school nuns got down to nightgowns and robes at 1:30 in the afternoon. Walking through the college dormitory, I used to feel as if I were walking through the pages of Thomas Mann's *Magic Mountain*. It looked for all the world like a nineteenth-century TB sanitarium, filled with willowy young consumptives stretched on beds or panting before hand fans as they listlessly attacked the omnipresent stack of books.

Even at night, custom prescribed a head covering. The hair was never to show. Some nuns wore soft wimples just like their day ones. The BVM's luckily wore little white cotton caps which made all of us novices giggle the first time we emerged in them looking like a row of Dutch-Cleanser dolls. One of our more hilarious postulant stories had to do with the unknowing late arrival who spotted a chair cover beside her bed and paraded down the corridor toward the shower with this strange object hanging from her worldly hairdo. Among the more austere elder nuns, I knew some who, from the day they were received, were never again seen except in full habit. (One such was a superior I once had who dressed in everything but her gloves just to answer the door after Solemn Silence!) Not all took the matter this seriously, of course. My most traumatic experience the first night at St. Joseph Academy was the sight of a large bald-headed fat man leaving the shower room as, eyes punctiliously lowered, I was about to enter. It took me one horrified moment to recognize old Sister Esmeralda who weighed a good two hundred, shaved her head in summer, and on suffocating August nights scorned to don a robe over her voluminous nightgown.

The moment one stepped into the habit, one lost a measure of individuality, of one's freedom to be oneself. In effect, one took on a corporate personality, a communal role. From this point on, whatever they did, wherever they went, novices were warned to view themselves not as persons but as representatives of a group. Cross your knees in public and you outraged Middle Catholicism. This public personality seemed to me the most difficult psychological effect of wearing a habit. Nuns had always to be "on the job." There was no moment of their lives when they were not the roles they played. "Father" got out on the golf course (if only in a loud, short-sleeved sport shirt over clerical pants), he got into a swimsuit, went out for dinner. Sister — never. Twenty-four hours a day she was frozen into her vocation. If you were Wordsworth's contemplative nun, this was bad enough. But if you were a graduate student plodding through inches of freezing early-morning rain toward your daily incarceration at the Library of Congress, it was unbearable.

I recall vividly the very moment when I knew that for twentieth-century nuns the habit had to go. It happened in Washington, D.C., at a windy intersection near Catholic University. One hand clutched a bulging briefcase; the other ran frantically after ten yards of serge set on ballooning about my head. Rain funneled down; the wind whipped my veil across my eyes. And at that instant the streetcar I'd been awaiting for twelve frozen minutes slid silently away without me. Sodden, chagrined, I would never awaken Wordsworth's muse. But I had been "conscienticized" to the need for change.

When the Vatican Council asked men and women religious to modernize their habits, a small group of us at Mundelein determined to work toward an experiment in contemporary dress. In innumerable rap sessions, we had come to view the religious habit primarily as a symbol of unfreedom. It helped to "fix" the nun in an exceptionally limited world. Like a belled cat, she had almost no mobility, no private personality. Sister Mary Elsa had come back from a Fulbright seminar in Paris the summer of 1960, delighted with the fact that French nuns had already begun to push back their coifs to reveal their hair. I saw her own attempts to imitate this tiny innovation nipped in the bud as one or another older BVM whispered in mildly scandalized tones, "Sister, your hairband has slipped up. Let me fix it." Elsa's familiar wail, "I can't even bend down to tie my shoe in public without attracting attention!" became the unofficial rallying cry for our program of radical change. And six years later, Elsa quite appropriately became one of the first BVM's to experiment with modern dress.

Pope Pius XII had paved the way for this radical change in Catholic tradition when, back in the fifties, he had asked nuns to adopt simpler, more comfortable habits in keeping with modern times.

Most communities, including my own, had responded by designing smaller headdresses, slimmer skirts, shorter veils. For reasons primarily aesthetic, skirts remained ankle-length. And it was a standing joke in ecclesiastical circles that only the initiate could detect modifications in the nuns' attire. Most nuns, it turned out, were deeply attached to their habits and didn't want any change at all. By the mid-sixties, when the Council again suggested an *aggiornamento,* the pressures for change had been long abuilding. In an avalanche of articles on the matter of religious dress, the debate swirled into public view and divided camps emerged.

Those who opposed contemporary dress for nuns pointed most often to traditional symbolism. Nuns had always been a visible sign of grace in a world conspicuously without it. Like the dinner jacket an Englishman donned to dine in the tropics, the habit, though inconvenient and anachronistic, was fringed with associations suggestive of moral and spiritual superiority. It elicited respect for its wearer. It surrounded her with an aura of mystery and distance which lifted the thoughts of an observer to an "eschatological plane," reminding him of final things he might prefer to forget. And there were a thousand other reasons why nuns ought not to discard the habit. The expense of keeping up with changing fashion, for one. The possible loss of group solidarity. Even a loss of modesty. A miniskirted nun was simply a contradiction in terms!

Shooting down such arguments was not easy, for attachment to cultural and religious symbols has deep emotional roots. Laughter helped somewhat. Most Americans had at one time or another landed in a subway or movie theater seat smack behind the flamboyant white sails of a nun's headdress. And every parochial school child understood the ambiguity of the habit. If a symbol of holiness, it was also a symbol of holy terror, an overwhelming sign of authority. This was the symbolism school principals and pastors intuitively invoked when they sent the rowdies "to Sister" for correction, not to the lay teacher. There was no question that the habit did operate as a kind of superpersonality, the dress itself taking on the properties of the state of life related to it. As long as the nuns projected an image tied to clothing, they were helpless to avoid such exploitation.

Originally, the nun's garb and the monk's habit had been merely the customary dress of the twelfth- or thirteenth-century upper classes. To remind the wearer of his vocation, his practice of Christian poverty, it was made in somber colors of less sumptuous materials. In court circles, styles changed. In cloistered ones, they did not. So, in time, the tunic, the cowl, the veil took on a symbolic character totally unrelated to their initial design. BVM's, a modern congregation founded in Philadelphia in 1833, had long known that their habit derived from the simple dress of Irish immigrant women who customarily dressed in black, wore long protective aprons, wrapped themselves in shawls, and bought the typical sun bonnet of the time to which eventually they attached a mourning veil when outside the house. Only the fact that the town female drunk came reeling out of a Dubuque tavern in a frilled cap exactly like the nuns' own led Bishop Hennessy to order our foundress to design for the Sisters a less attractive headdress.

Though she complied by putting her Sisters into a kind of Quaker bonnet which totally hid the hair, Mary Frances Clarke herself never wore any kind of habit. And had not the bishop insisted, the rest of the community probably would not have done so either. But a nineteenth-century male-oriented Church handed women religious a code of canon law prescribing in detail not only the minutiae of their lives but the minutiae of their dress. To modern American nuns, such restrictions began to appear for what they were — silent witness to the domination-oppression syndrome operative in the Church since the fifth century. In the 1960's it seemed demeaning to us that women religious should have to submit details of their change of habit to male members of the Congregation for Religious. And a top official of the National Conference of Major Religious Superiors agreed that Cardinal Ildebrando Antoniutti had bigger problems to worry about than nuns' hemlines. "I really want to needle him," admitted Father B. L. Wittenbrink, O.M.I., permanent secretary of the conference. "Experimentation is the law of life — adapt or perish. We didn't invent it, by the way; it's God's law."

The Council had asked religious congregations to rethink and redesign their habits in the spirit of *aggiornamento*. It wisely did not specify precisely how this was to be done. It suggested only faithfulness to the mind of the founder of the religious orders and to their unique aim. Obviously it was the mind of our foundress that her Sisters wear the dress of the day so that they might mingle inconspicuously with parishioners in that rough little mining town out in the Territory of Iowa. How had that original, simple black dress evolved into the medieval-looking garb we wore in 1967 — long flowing sleeves, tight inner sleeves, voluminous skirts of fine French serge, delicate veils? Obviously, with the help of an outmoded canonical code, we had been moving backwards with all possible speed.

The Institute on Problems that Unite Us, the self-study which followed on its heels, and the determined lobbying we set in motion convinced top administrators of the BVM congregation that only through experimentation could the General Chapter scheduled to meet in 1969 gather the data it would need to make changes in the direction of renewal. On February 22, 1966, Mother Mary Consolatrice informed the congregation that she was launching a fact-finding experiment with regard to dress. This would involve modification of the traditional habit, the introduction of a completely modern habit, and experiment with contemporary dress. She wanted chapter delegates to have something more substantial than their personal likes and dislikes to help them arrive at decisions.

We learned with surprise that a BVM doctoral student at the University of Minnesota had been wearing secular dress since the previous March: her teaching assistantship depended on it. Two nuns at Mundelein were also to be given permission to wear secular dress — one to work as a clinical psychologist, one to experiment at the college. Excitement crackled through the community: the nose of the camel was under the tent! By August, eight of us at Mundelein had "come out." And what a funny, exhilarating experience it was. Our numbers grew rapidly. Every other day someone else would emerge. Reassurances buoyed up fainthearted converts. ("You look marvelous, really! No one would ever guess!") Actually, for a time, *everyone* guessed. For days we continued to reach for non-existent long habits as we started up or down stairs. You could tell a nun instantly from the way she teased or didn't tease her hair, the way she self-consciously wrapped her bare arms in a sweater however hot the day, the way she tugged at skirts designed to display, not conceal, the knees.

With wicked delight, our students discovered that, despite those flawless complexions, lots of us were middle-aged. For a while, no

Catholic woman of any chic would be caught wearing a dark suit with a white blouse. And black trench coats were definitely passé. But after a few hilarious reactions, nuns did stop smiling indiscriminately at all comers. Bright colors appeared; miniskirts raised a few eyebrows; unsuspected personalities surfaced as we grew less self-aware, more used to being ourselves. Nuns continued to have a kind of Westchester housewife look. But imperceptibly that too vanished. The day an intern at St. Francis Hospital stepped aside to allow a habited nurse to exit from the elevator, then shoved ahead of two Mundelein nuns in normal dress, they stared at each other in triumph. They had finally "passed" in the outside world.

Attending the American Council on Education meeting in New Orleans, I discovered what fun it was getting about without a veil. In a pouring rain I jumped into a cab with Esther Rauschenbush, the acting president of Sarah Lawrence College. As we exchanged names, I saw her eyes widen. A moment of hesitation, then —"Did you say Sister?" she asked, incredulously taking in my oyster gray wool-knit suit, makeup (subdued, but there), earrings. When I cheerfully admitted who I was, she smiled. "I think it's *marvelous*. May I ask how long you'd worn the habit?"

"Twenty-seven years."

"And how long have you been in modern dress?"

"A month."

"And how long did it take to get used to it?"

"Oh — about twenty minutes."

Actually, taking off the habit was considerably easier than putting it on. After all, I'd worn normal dress for twenty-two years before I entered. And short skirts were far less of a challenge than floor-length ones.

The stories of such encounters were legion and frequently very funny. A group of unenthusiastic Catholic women, lunching in the next booth at the Conrad-Hilton while the American Association for Higher Education meeting was in progress, proved their one-upmanship by identifying every hapless nun they spotted. "My dear, you can tell them a mile away. They're so *dowdy*." On the instant, Dick Saunders, fellow board member, discovered me and planted a teasing kiss on my cheek as he announced, "Sister, you look wonderful. I've been wanting to do this for years!" (I did *not* resist a glance at the next table as we exited arm in arm.) A reassuring anecdote in *Women's Wear Daily* described a man getting on an elevator and asking three young women in blue uniforms what order they belonged to. Their reply: "We're airline stewardesses!"

Actually, my comment to Mrs. Rauschenbush was an accurate one. Though to the general public there was something delightfully novel in seeing nuns looking just like everyone else, most nuns took the change in stride. A few BVM's persisted in wearing short shoulder-length veils, a kind of vestigial habit which assured their being identified. And for a time all of us wore veils in chapel. But these were so clearly anachronistic that they disappeared by common consent. It was better to be one thing or the other. Some nuns in our congregation preferred the traditional habit. A few wear it to this moment. For the most part, however, American nuns now dress like the professional women they are. They themselves find it hard to believe that less than a decade ago they were encumbered in quaint, medieval habits, the great white wings which today only Brooks Costume Company preserves.

Discarding the habit had more significant psychological than sartorial meaning. And it made a unique contribution to an evolving theology of religious life. Traditionally, nuns had withdrawn from the world. Their dress spoke of cloister and seclusion. When they changed their names, their garb, their manner of life, they symbolized the distance they meant to place between themselves and the outside world. In the wake of Vatican II, nuns opted unequivocally *for* the world. Their choice was grounded not in a theology of withdrawal but in one of involvement. This is really what getting into contemporary dress was all about. It wasn't the only return to normality; it was just the most dramatic.

To reemphasize the importance of baptism, the Sacred Congregation of Religious had fortunately several years earlier given nuns the option of resuming their family names. So all those nuns who had taken a father's or a brother's or some favorite male saint's name on Reception day could now shed "George" or "James" or "John" before they got back into nylons!

If you liked your given name, you happily went back to being Frances Shea (instead of Sister Mary Frances Patricia) or Helen Wright (Mother Mary Consolatrice). If you preferred your religious one, you kept it and went on being Sister Elsa Copeland. If, like me, you *hated* the original (Agnes) and couldn't stand the present (Ignatia), you cleverly just kept Mary and tried to reeducate your friends. And you ended up in a traumatic loss of identity that is not to be believed! Nothing, I've discovered, could matter less than one's preference regarding names. Shakespeare had it all wrong. A rose by any other name is totally unacceptable.

As always, Marion had the first word. "Your mother gave you that name. If it was good enough for her, it's good enough for me, Agnes."

My nieces followed suit. "But, Aunt *Tag-nes*. Mary doesn't *sound* like you!"

My friends were either incensed ("But I don't *want* to change your name!") or hilarious about the matter. On a trip to Cuernavaca, Jane Trahey was determined to make a fresh start, and she tried at every opportunity. "This is — uh — my friend — uh-uh — Mary," I heard her saying lamely as I glanced around at a party to see who it was she was introducing. "Mary Griffin," she added firmly before we both broke down in helpless laughter. "I can't help it, Naish," she confessed later. "I keep thinking, 'Who in God's name is *Mary?*'"

Today at Pratt Avenue I continue to be "Natia"; Joan Frances is still J.F., and Mary De Cock (she hated Helen and foolishly stuck with Mary too) is forever Donatus. When the telephone rings, we identify the caller by the worlds our names represent. I hear J.F. asking innocently, "Mary D. or Mary G.?" and I know there's a nun on the line. "Naish" means my pals. "Agnes"— it's the family. "Mary Griffin"— it's a stranger calling!

The return to our Christian names, the return to ordinary dress, the return to normal modes of life — all have narrowed the gap between the nun and the world. Vatican II explicitly asserted the importance of the lay Christian. It denied that religious life was in any sense a "higher" one. And it has reinforced this concept with some of the most powerful clothes philosophy since Carlyle's.

CHAPTER SIX

LOWERING THE DRAWBRIDGE

There is in fact only one religion from which the concept of community is inseparable, and that is Christianity.

— DIETRICH VON BONHOEFFER

Sociologists call them "small, intentional groups." The nuns themselves refer to "apartment living." Whatever the term, the reality is that small, self-chosen living groups are rapidly displacing the old-style conventual community once gathered together by appointment of the provincial and traditionally called a "house" or a "mission." From California to New York, men and women religious, Jesuits, Dominicans, Sisters of Charity, have launched such a spate of experiments in community that early in 1970 a Washington, D.C., workshop in experimental living was crammed with delegates from the orders trying to get a bead on what was emerging.

I myself never got to Washington. In fact I had not so much as heard that there was such a meeting. I was still picking up the pieces after that first wonderful Christmas at Pratt Avenue. With four other BVM's, I had moved from Mundelein into an apartment on Chicago's North Side in late summer of 1969.

We'd tried hard to get some variety as well as congeniality into the group. When, amid half-uncrated books and yawning suitcases, we called a halt for hamburgers and Schlitz that hot August night of our arrival, we smugly agreed that we had a fair scatter — two profs from Mundelein, a math teacher from Kendall College, an ex-provincial turned high-school administrator, and a Ph.D. candidate in social ethics.

All of us had lived together in the community at Mundelein. Most of us had been friends for more years than we publicly admitted to. All had been deeply involved in bringing about change in the congregation as a whole. We thought alike about dress (it should be contemporary); about prayer (it should be unscheduled and informal); about money (it should be pooled); about living (it should be simple, human, and free). We disagreed vociferously about politics and politicians — academic, ecclesiastical, and national. We found ourselves on a widely spread continuum when it came to schedules and housekeeping. (We had, we discovered, our compulsive and our casual life-stylists.) Eventually we learned that living together on intimate terms reveals one not only to others, willy-nilly, but to oneself as well. And that such honesty, if bracing, can also be very painful. That first little group didn't survive as a permanent community. But all of us grew up in it. We hadn't expected paradise regained. Like all Utopia planners, we had merely aimed at the "good" life. In some respects it eluded us. But for the most part we found it.

From Plato through More through *Walden II,* Utopias have been misunderstood as attempts at "perfect" societies. Their creators considered them ideal only in the sense that they existed as imaginative constructs, as ideas, not as practical experiments. Indeed, Thomas More was careful to point out that Hythlodaye's City of Shadows had a built-in limitation: it was only as perfect as unaided human reason could make it. But Christianity was on the horizon for the Utopians; there was hope of a more perfect society to come. In the thirteenth century St. Thomas Aquinas, in his *Summa Theologica*, had considered the viability of communal living and concluded that only where there is a religious impulse is communism apt to work, since what belongs to everyone belongs to no one and men are apt to care only for that in which they have a personal stake. The continuance of the monastic orders into the twentieth century alongside the failure of the Oneidas, the Brook Farms, the Hopedales, the Fruitlands thus far proves Thomas a prophet. But the desire to build a better life is a perennial one. The disillusionment of the sixties rekindled the communal impulse in America. Alongside hundreds of communes which mushroomed across the land, a determined little group led by Kathleen Kinkaid brought B. F. Skinner's behavioral ideas to life in Fair Oaks, Virginia, perhaps the most famous of modern experiments. At Fair Oaks, disagreements over government led to tensions and confrontation and to eventual "departure of the rebels." Pratt Avenue too was to experience dissension and separation. In many respects we've proved to be more like Fair Oaks than not

There was a crucial difference between these two groups, however. Surprisingly, it had to do with candidness. When at Fair Oaks Hal threatened to destroy the lease and kick the commune off his land, confrontation was ugly but it was out in the open. When our Pratt Avenue group polarized, we found ourselves unable to face our interactional problems.

Usually you didn't even know that anything was wrong except for an elaborate courtesy which subtly replaced the normal give and take. Then doors were quietly closed; silences grew; coolness rose like a chilling mist. Had we had the courage at such times to face the issue squarely, had we even had the good sense to bring in a facilitator when group relations badly deteriorated, we might have made it intact through that first year. Instead, incredibly naïve about group process, we bungled badly. Our introspective lives had obviously made us very understanding about our own foibles, very intolerant about those of others.

Certainly Pratt Avenue had no monopoly on problems. Other groups had their fair share. And we all lived too close together not to know about them. The house car was a common thorn. Once it had been someone's father the nuns used to call for a ride. Now the driver was right there in the house and found herself exploited just as ruthlessly. When the worm turned, a lot of learner's permits began to appear. Then there was the problem of the bathroom. Everyone was loath to put up a sign: "All of us use this room. Let's keep it clean." It seemed too much like living on a DC 10. But we did have our slobs who didn't pick up the towels, didn't mind unmade beds or sticky jam jars. And in a small group you knew who they were.

In one house the crisis came over washing the dog's face with a dish towel. ("He's a snarling, unfriendly pain-in-the-neck, anyway. So we laid it on the line.") There were the fanatical neateners, forever ironing the permanent-press table mats, bent on turning the family dinner table into a replica of the convent altar. When the nuns protested freezing temperatures in one apartment, their rat-fink landlord countered by suggesting that Sisters should be used to mortification. There were physical fitness nuts who took over the living room for yoga or ballet practice. There were Mancini devotees in a den of Bach lovers. There was the lady who lived above all mundane housekeeping tasks, sitting specterlike behind the *Sun Times* in the living room: you hardly knew she was home unless you saw her shadow! Another had a way of dodging the weekly junket to the supermarket; left her breakfast dishes for the next of kin; eternally forgot to fill in the stubs in the community checkbook. In short, once out of the showcase of institutional life, nuns turned out to be delightfully and maddeningly human. And not terribly good at dealing with each other in such close quarters. The years of enforced silence, seclusion, and duty lists had left their mark. Traditional religious life had fostered a carefully guarded privacy. But this very sense of apartness left us, I suspect, quite unprepared for the openness intentional communities demand. Those of us who wanted out of institutional living, who pressed for the opportunity to experiment, did so no doubt for a thousand separate reasons. But one of the chief reasons we gave each other was to escape the atmosphere of isolation we found there.

In the convent you could live side by side with another Sister for years, face her across breakfast and dinner tables for ten thousand silent meals, exchange the most inane small talk with her during enforced recreation periods, pray beside her in chapel, even take your turn as night nurse when the inevitable surgery punctuated her life — and you could remain total strangers to each other. The loneliness of secularized urban man was familiar to nuns and priests. The Jesuit found dead in his room after three days was legendary among religious. The eccentrics among us who withdrew over the years — first for the convenient headache which demanded "going to bed early," finally for an alienation which demanded going to the motherhouse early — were not unfamiliar phenomena. Man was not meant to live alone. But he also was not meant to be "institutionalized." The formal manner nuns so often adopted with others, the web of privacy they wove about themselves, the territorial imperatives senior members exhibited ("my" pew, "my" TV program, "my" classroom) — these seemed a kind of protective coloration total institutions produced. One could not live on intimate terms with sixty other persons. One adapted by presenting either a public or a personal mask to "meet the faces one would meet." So we measured out our lives in school and meeting rooms. Apartment living seemed a blue front in a gray sky. It promised an unprecedented freedom. Freedom to develop a life-style of our own; freedom to deal with poverty (and money) realistically; freedom to extend our community to friends and new neighbors; freedom to pray in ways comfortable to us; freedom to get away from our work environment; freedom just to *be*. In that heady time, when to be alive seemed very Heaven, I don't recall adverting to the fact that I was taking the same old institution-shaped personality along with me!

The six-room Pratt Avenue apartment is a big rambling affair which runs the length of the first floor in a sixty-year-old red-brick flat building east of Sheridan Road and almost on the beach. Its somewhat fading charms were enhanced both by its nearness to the college (a five-minute walk) and the fact that another group of BVM's was leaving it for a larger apartment after only a year's stay. We inherited not only a convent-clean house but such invaluable accouterments as third-hand draperies, rusty radiator covers, built-in bookshelves, and tenuous plywood desks constructed on the premises by the previous occupants. Unencumbered with furniture, we accepted everything, rejected nothing on the tacit assumption that we could sort it all out later. Aside from our view of Lake Michigan, the greatest aesthetic advantage I saw in the house was its brightness and openness. The living room had a wood-burning fireplace fronted by an old fire screen, the kitchen had a catch-all porch at its back, and a garage came with the house. The plumbing worked most of the time; the light gray wall-to-wall carpeting looked quite splendid as the light waned. Our collection of college-loaned or rejected beds and chairs and lamps fleshed out with family-contributed end tables, odd dishes, and a marvelous reclining chair that had belonged to Mary De Cock's Uncle Jim fell together like inmates of an old country house. We had more rocking chairs than the Kennedy compound and no dining room table at all. But we entertained Jane Trahey, our very first guest, with New York strip steaks and bad wine served on a borrowed metal sewing table of disquieting tremulousness with as much éclat as Jane said her mama would have attributed to Mrs. Potter Palmer.

But Mrs. Potter Palmer had something going for her that we did not — namely, lots of money. And it didn't take us long to discover that New York strip steak on Saturday night meant Elsa's Hamburger Helper the next, and perhaps the next! Threatened with a sea of hamburger, we fled to budget-making. And for people with a vow of poverty, who literally had not had a red cent to their names for years, this proved a novel experience.

The vow of poverty, I should explain, did not ordinarily mean a life of deprivation. Its purpose was to detach. The spirit of poverty is the direct antithesis of the spirit of greed. The hope is that one will find one's treasure, as did Christ, in Heaven. Unencumbered by gold (or the desire for it) the nun travels light and therefore fast. She takes literally the Gospel injunction, "Sell what thou hast, give to the poor and come follow me." Viewed thus, poverty is a splendid kind of freedom. It makes one mobile, flexible, incorruptible. Like Thoreau, one wanders happily along the aisles of Bonwit Teller's viewing with delight all the things one has neither the means nor the desire to buy.

But if the nun handled no money (save for the limited amount she requested for city travel or for small personal needs), a lot of money was spent on her. The community called this the "hundred-fold," for the Rule indicated that superiors were to see to it that the nuns were warmly (if simply) housed, decently clad, wholesomely nourished. Their medical needs must be met, their professional expenses are budgeted for. They are decently buried in community plots for which "perpetual care" has been arranged. Until very recently their retirement was assured by the contributions of younger members who in turn could count on the "living endowment" of those coming after them. In the post–Vatican II drift away from religious life, however, the median age of nuns has risen sharply and funds for retirement have become a critical concern. When an order of Dominican nuns in Houston, Texas, applied for old-age assistance in December, 1972, a shock wave of reaction hit the Catholic community. Americans United for Separation of Church and State also reacted, characteristically pointing out that since the nuns had paid no taxes and it was the Church which had benefited by their labors all those giving years, the Church should now assume responsibility for them, not the state. Interestingly enough, this is the view the nuns themselves support and through the Leadership Conference of Women Religious have presented to the American hierarchy. Diocese by diocese, bishops are beginning to contribute to retirement costs of nuns once stationed there. In addition, having successfully pressed for inclusion under the Social Security System, some 150,000 nuns now have the option of building up Social Security benefits at retirement. Together with indications that nuns are slowly moving toward their goal of full salaries for professional work, these changes brighten the economic picture for American nuns generally.

When, in 1968, the Mundelein religious community, having debated every inch of the way, decided to launch experiments in small-group living, every one of us came to grips with the matter of finances. The costs of housing the nuns were extracted from the college budget and translated into dollars and cents. Estimating what was spent for food, clothing, medicine, upkeep of community cars, and so on, we found that we averaged out at $195.00 a sister per month. Eureka — our budget, $2,340.00 a year, to be paid in twelve monthly installments. And we were to be totally on our own.

("You mean we have to pay for lunch if we drop into the college dining room?" "You bet!")

Gathered around our dining-sewing table to plan Pratt Avenue finances, we found we were in fairly good shape. Certainly we were not affluent. But neither were we the risky venture a lot of hippie communes were. Margaret Dolan, an administrator at St. Mary's Center for Learning, was taking a minimum salary from that struggling alternative school. Her income about matched our own. Cecilia, full-time at Kendall, was the only full-salaried member of the group. But she opted to live on the same amount as the rest of us. To function as a community, we agreed, meant to act in concert and make what impact we could. In this spirit we decided to withhold our federal taxes from the telephone company as an antiwar protest. And we shot off a letter telling them of this fact. Feeling a little like Thoreau beginning his frugal ledger at Walden and registering his small protest against the Mexican War, we spelled out our considerably more lush expense account. From each of us $110.00 monthly into the common fund for rent, utilities, food, small personal supplies. To each $85.00 a month for all other needs — clothing, medicine, books, travel, and so forth. Gas for the Volks would come out of the common fund (we'd all pile into Mary De Cock's vintage bug whenever possible). Repairs on the car would come out of her graduate school loan. And the Providence of God, it was hoped, would kindly hold these to a minimum. We opened a joint checking account, learned by trial and error to balance our statements, and felt ourselves launched into the Real World. Financially, at least, we were responsible for ourselves.

"Radix malorum est cupiditas," warned Chaucer's Pardoner. It wasn't the love of money, however, that proved for us the root of all evil. It was love of spending the Common Fund after one's own designs. When Cecilia shopped, the larder filled up with tuna fish, corn flakes, canned peas — all to reappear later in the mouth-watering entrees from the hand of the Casserole Queen. ("So *fattening!*" we groaned over second helpings.) When Margaret shopped, we ran to standing rib roasts, Kosher corned beef, Levy's rye, hand-packed ice cream. ("So *fattening* and *expensive*," the rest of us wailed, relishing the last scraps of savory pink beef). "Let's have a happy hour just on Friday nights," I suggested in a burst of virtue. (And they accused me of packing the week with Fridays.) Elsa rebelled against such vin ordinaire as Gallo; Donatus against perpetual garbage detail ("So learn to cook" came the cheerful salvo). In the long run, the budget itself — impervious, inflexible — set priorities for us. The outcome was predictable; if one night we had barbecued shrimp and Soave Bolla, the next three featured hamburgers, tacos, or frozen turbot. When we hit the bottom of the barrel, there was always Turkish moussaka. There were, we had discovered, one hundred ways to fix squash (ninety involving ground meat).

There were other ways of managing money, we discovered. The nuns at 1123 Pratt (just beyond the Rabbi's house) each put $125.00 into their fund. On Kenmore they tossed the whole thing into the kitty, then just took out what they needed for personal expenses. Cecilia had wanted us to consider her monthly check part of our common fund and to make shared decisions regarding its use. We argued the matter pro and con and decided against it. The feeling was that, even if we never used the money, just *having* that bank balance would make for an unrealistic security. The threat of overdrawing the family account was a very real one.

So Cecilia worked out her own arrangements with the motherhouse. But when she bought for Pratt Avenue a much-needed washer and dryer, she insisted that someone else help her select it. "It's not mine; it's ours," she pointed out. And, a year later, as she left Pratt

Avenue and religious life as well, the almost new Lady Kenmore equipment stayed behind where it splashes and gurgles away still.

To have shared *all* our resources would have meant taking a primitive Christian approach to community: from each according to his ability, to each according to his need. But this would have demanded utter openness to each other — no personal cache for a rainy day; no quietly accumulating little nest egg (we all picked up occasional extra income from honoraria, moonlighting, and so on) against some summer Grand Tour, some pet charitable project, some dramatic accession to one's wardrobe. These were, after all, the limitations within which all of us had lived our traditional conventual lives. That most of us now wanted some control over some miniscule corner of our financial souls came as no surprise to me. Making personal choices, however tiny, is a necessary function of being a person. And this freedom so to choose was apparently too new, too hard-won, too precious to be relinquished to even so glowing an ideal as perfect community. We kept our personal checking accounts. And with them one tiny segment of our lives wherein each of us is sole and responsible proprietor.

In many ways, money is central to the success of the new life-styles nuns are developing in the seventies. Those of us living in apartments (there are about a hundred in the Chicago area alone) realize that we have a job of public education to do. In 1968 the most common argument raised against group living was its expense. Wasn't it cheaper to live in college housing? In parish-owned convents? Cost analysis revealed that the answer was very often a surprising no. Six nuns rattling around in a massive, old-fashioned convent built for twenty are manifestly costing a parish more than it bargains for. Lived in or not, the whole house must be heated, cleaned, tuck-pointed, painted. And the parish will ordinarily supply a car, pay for insurance and upkeep. In the long run, dioceses might be better off to pay Sisters a professional salary and let them look after their own housing and retirement costs. Pastors could then stop being landlords and nuns could start being responsible citizens.

At Mundelein we discovered that college housing and food costs easily matched those of apartment dwellers. Overhead costs of elevator operation, food service, and building maintenance necessarily are reflected in convent expenses. When the nuns occupy sections of the college building, there is simply no way to separate these out.

Aware of the high cost of institutional living, some pastors are themselves initiating changes by turning convents into parish centers, raising the stipends of the teaching Sisters, and asking them to move into apartments. Even administrators of religious congregations, which a few years ago were permitting only the narrowest kind of experimentation with housing, have seen the financial foolhardiness of maintaining a large convent for a handful of nuns. At St. Mary's Center for Learning in Chicago, BVM's were this past September asked by their own community to find other housing, as their spacious, recently built convent was being leased to the Illinois State Medical Center. When such official action is taken by a religious order, it is clear that the experiment is over: apartment living has been recognized as a viable alternative. Soon such communes may in fact be the only alternative open to nuns. Already the novelty of such a life-style has worn off for the general public. The mailman no longer looks suspicious when a petite brunette in shorts signs for a registered letter addressed to Sister Joan Frances Crowley. The nuns get ticketed for parking on the wrong side of the street ("And he knew it was our beat-up Volks too!"). The neighbors are used to hearing Catholic hymns drifting through an open window when a priest occasionally offers the liturgy in the living room. Though his son stretches a cord between our houses to separate off the goyim, the Rabbi drops in on Christmas Eve, and the janitor expects "the usual" at the holiday season. Even the usher halts the Sunday collection plate in front of the nuns. ("They look like human beings, don't they?") And *nobody* gets up to give Sister a seat in the subway any more. Lord, it's nice being anonymous!

But solving our money problems, solving our housing problems doesn't by any means solve the problem of just plain living together. However congenial the groups that form, however hard they work at it — communal living takes constant maintenance. If the apartment is small, privacy becomes a priceless commodity. Sharing it can at times seem a matter of heroism. At those moments, one escapes to whatever haven offers — a movie, dinner out, the college library, one's campus office. Radios blare when you want quiet; the crowd wants "The FBI" when you want "Masterpiece Theater." The night you planned to do your hair is the night three people bring someone home for dinner.

Still, no one ever talks about "offering it up" any more, thank God. You give a little; you take a little. When people find they can't make it in one group, they try another. Or they go back to institutional living. If you take a job elsewhere, you put up with the inconvenience of commuting, or you leave the nest. But it's not the end of the world. We all moved in with people we thought were compatible. Sometimes they weren't. But then it's hard for any people to live together. Nuns are no exception.

When the group does make it, however, it's a delight. The night you get into O'Hare an hour late and find the faithful little Volks still steaming past the Delta terminal in sub-zero weather; the day your niece drops in with five under six and someone conjures up a miraculous draft of hamburgers and shakes; the nights you argue and laugh the end of the day away over dinner it wasn't your turn to make — these are the moments when you know what the new hundredfold of community is. And you wouldn't go back for anything.

There are, of course, pitfalls to small-group living. You can end up with people totally wrong for you. (They zing when you zang!) You can fall into the bourgeois trap — cultivate a suburban housewife look; begin to accumulate books, tape recorders, cameras; forget about sharing in a world filled with want. But none of these is unique to a commune. Institutional life too breeds hoarders, throws the wrong people together, makes for a dependence on paid personal services, isolates and insulates. All things being equal, there's something to be said for the leveling effect of taking out the garbage. There was garbage in the convent too. I don't forget that. But there was a superior to decide who got to dump it. Here, *we* decide. And that's perhaps the biggest change of all — the most radical break with tradition and orthodoxy. For, after cost, the second greatest objection outsiders had to apartment living was our announced intention to experiment with group decision making. How could you have nuns without a superior?

The Vatican Council helped here. Its emphasis on collegiality and subsidiarity had instant resonance for religious communities. The first meant shared decision making (the allusion was primarily to the bishops and lay Catholics); the second meant grass-roots self-governance (especially at the parish and diocesan levels).

As a member of the 1968 Chapter Commission on Government, I had supported a motion for the most surprising innovation to date. It called for the suspension of the powers of all local superiors (those heading individual houses) and an experiment in self-government wherever the Sisters wished it. Superiors weren't really liquidated. If a house wanted one, it could vote her back in. Otherwise, the nuns were free to farm out administrative jobs to members of the group or get along with unstructured chaos. All the local houses — whether convents or apartments — were asked to pick a community representative who could open official mail and deal with the pastor and the janitor. (How were the mighty fallen!)

After a month of getting the Pratt family on the road, when we stopped to take stock of ourselves, we admitted candidly that we'd never even noticed that the superior wasn't there. Three of the four of us had just finished out a term under Sister Mary Emily at Mundelein, in our opinion the best of all possible superiors. On reflection, we decided that, like certain lucky African nations, we'd been quietly prepared for post-colonial autonomy! Actually, over the years, the job of superior in our congregation had little by little been eroded. Superiors had long since ceased to appoint companions for travel. And not since the late nineteenth century had they asked for a "manifestation of conscience." Of course there were the diehards who kept a hawklike watch over minor infractions of the Rule, slit the incoming mail (so you never knew if it had been read), imposed some academic spiritual advice on the young. But for the most part superiors were good and useful people who worried about you when you were sick, spoiled you when you weren't, and in general gave a sense of cohesiveness to the house. Collegiality meant a governing of ourselves by consensus. Everyone in the group was equal to everyone else. And group solidarity deepened with friendship.

So we got down to the heady business of making our own decisions. Looked in the face, they were Lilliputian indeed.

Q. Shall we list the jobs to be done and sign up for a week at a time?

A. No! Down with the work concept. Everyone knows what needs to be done. Just do your thing.

Q. Shall we dine early or late? Have a long evening to study or a short one to relax?

A. Late as we can. Dinner at 5:00 is *barbarous.*

Q. What about guests? Check with the group ahead of time?

A. *Heavens!* this is *home.* Bring 'em along.

Q. Pray together?

A. When we feel like it.

Q. Save Green Stamps?

A. You bet!

Thus the New Life began — but with what a sense of freedom, joy in each other, delight in self-discovery I cannot find words to say. All the expected things happened, and a few quite unlooked for. For a while we were very beatnicky — leaving beds unmade, who had mitered corners for a quarter of a century. Watching the dust build up where once it was boasted, "You could eat off the floors." For a while we were inundated with friends, then friends of friends who seemingly swarmed out of the woodwork to see what we were up to. I vividly recall a phone which rang incessantly and TV newscasters who for all practical purposes just moved in and took over the living room. For a while all of us were uptight about the whole matter of guests. But suddenly we realized that we didn't have to suspend operations whenever someone dropped in. People might actually like some privacy! It might be nice to clear out after dinner.

Serenity is not easily bought. And apartment living owns no special magic to conjure it into being. Eventually all groups, whatever their makeup, come to see that they have to build in their own brand of discipline. Luckily we all have jobs. And they take us in different directions. We all have friends outside the group. We all have interests which give us more than one dimension. But living in the group has given us a home, has made Pratt Avenue Fair Oaks for Elsa, J.F., Donatus, and me. It was for this we freed ourselves from the dead hand of institution, for this we lowered the draw-bridge and crossed the moat into the Real World of leaky plumbing, menu planning, lost garage keys. We are not apt to cross back.

CHAPTER SEVEN

TOPA: FREE AT LAST!

POVERTY
Sister Mary joined the poor this fall;
1) *her small apartment's old sometimes cold:*
   and
2) *when the wind blows she recalls her coat was*
   cheap;
3) *to eat she spends a bit on soup and sales:*
   and
4) *she has learned to stay in after eight.*
Don't let her think she knows the whole of
poverty — she knows she can get out.
                              — JUDY WASHBUSH
                         Sisters Today, October, 1972

Getting out of Chicago is predictable: the Dan Ryan clogged with exhaust-spewing behemoths, our rented car weaving audaciously from lane to lane. In Cairo we pull up in front of a Chinese restaurant for a quick supper of chicken subgum and eggrolls. Too late we find ourselves a somewhat scruffy island in a sea of ladies with spun-sugar hair and harried spouses. We've hit Cairo's Pump Room on a Saturday night.

Cross the river at Cairo and pick up Interstate 55, heading for Arkansas in a blinding downpour. It's sheer heaven to fall into bed in Memphis sometime after midnight. The BVM's have a house there and they've prepared against our coming with plenty of ice-cold beer and a stock of marvelous stories. In the morning we make a thoughtful pilgrimage to The Lorraine, the somewhat garrish motel where, incredibly, Martin Luther King was shot in April of 1968. We stand on the balcony. We look toward the window where James Earl Ray had taken aim. But it is still too fresh in our memories and we leave quickly. Our guide points out Elvis Presley's mansion with its guard house, its wrought-iron gates surmounted by an enormous musical note. Images of King and Presley dance incongruously in my mind.

We're into Mississippi fast now and at Granada turn off on Route 7 to get a closer look at the terrain. It's prettier than I'd expected with pine and scrub oak and nameless other trees fringing the road. Outside Greenwood we miss our turn trying to pick up Route 43 and for the first time we see up close Mississippi's legendary poverty. The clapboard shanties are worse than those of Selma but the potholes are depressingly familiar.

Unpainted sagging porches, the startled round eyes of children crowding a doorway, an ancient black man, big-knuckled hands loose on blue-denimed knees. In Tchula more miserable shanties tilting awry on concrete-block stilts, set back from the highway on sunbaked unpaved streets. The houses huddle together, elbowing and jostling each other like big-city tenement flats. Not at all like the isolated plantation remnants we will see driving back north through Clarksdale. There tiny cabins string along the horizon. A dilapidated car rusts in the overgrown fields, an antediluvian washing machine clings to a slanting porch. Abandoned. Abandoned. Yet as one looks back from the highway, smoke trails from a crumbling chimney, tiny white shirts and blue jeans flap on the line behind the house, invisible children shriek at play. These are Mississippi's favelas, the sobering backdrop to Natchez's antebellum elegance so exquisitely preserved in Rosalie, Longwood, The Laurels. Long a closed society, Mississippi reveals itself still as a country of two cultures.

Highway 61 flows down to Natchez from Vicksburg. Midway in that ninety-mile stretch, just below Port Gibson (the town Grant found too pretty to burn on his way to the siege of Vicksburg) a red neon arrow directs us away from the highway and onto the seven-mile stretch of county road 552 which serpentines its way to the oldest black land-grant college in the country. In the dusky heat this two-lane road seems endless. We plunge toward the river, our head-lights picking out an occasional dirt road branching off into nothing-ness. A scrawny hound dog blinks at the roadside; stray goats scramble away. The road curves sharply and a battered pickup looms ahead, a hunting gun riding the rack behind the driver. Chilled, I remember that this is the country of Andrew Goodman, Michael Schwerner, James Chaney. Five years before, they had disappeared at Philadelphia, Mississippi. A lonely country road. Civil rights workers. We pick up courage and speed, and pass the pickup. The driver lifts a casual hand in greeting. Then suddenly there are lights. We rumble over the cattle guard. A sign announces, "Alcorn Agri-cultural and Mechanical College."

Going to Alcorn in the fall of 1970 was a response-able decision on my part. It was my way of responding to perceived needs, in Niebuhr's sense of the term. I applied to Mundelein for a leave of absence. I applied to the congregation for permission to live "out-side the community." In both instances I met with the fullest sup port. But by the time I was ready to take off from Pratt Avenue, all this network of permissions was already outmoded. TOPA (totally open personnel application) had just been officially adopted by the community senate. From now on, BVM's would no longer be de-ployed like troops. From now on, responding to the needs of the world as they saw them, they would themselves largely determine the direction of the congregational apostolate. TOPA was the pivot which made this unprecedented swing toward free choice possible. In many ways, it was the most radical change BVM's had yet effected.

Within the classic framework of the vow of obedience, nuns did not choose their jobs, they were assigned them. August 15 was traditionally "D Day" in the community — the day your letter of appointment arrived. If you were being changed — sent to another mission, assigned to full-time graduate study, retired to the mother-house — this was the day on which the news broke, to you as well as to everybody else. And the community custom was to have your trunk packed by the previous night so that, if you "got a letter," you could leave by the next train, the next car, the next boat! Even superiors who were finishing their term of office tried to clear out before their successors arrived. It was considered bad form to hang around after your replacement came. One was to obey with alacrity, to get out as soon as possible. This was considered "cheerful" compliance — an ideal by no means universally attained; for sometimes changes came after one had worked in a given situation for years, had put down roots. What one was leaving was not only a job but friends, a community, a way of life. "Detachment" was the name of the game. Certainly superiors tried hard to consider the natural abilities of their subjects and encouraged them to make difficult or unbearable situations known. But, all things being equal, they had to satisfy the demands of the market. If Sputnik decreed that scientists were in high demand, if a large number of music teachers happened to reach retirement in a given year, if interest in home economics suddenly burgeoned, the provincial and the director of education might put their heads together over the academic qualifications of the next group of novices to be professed and change a few academic majors in the process. I knew of a novice who had studied piano for years before she entered but never once touched the keyboard after that for fear that some provincial would make her a music teacher!

Curiously enough, this rather prehistoric way of directing careers often enough proved quite successful. And it frequently opened up to nuns educational opportunities quite out of the question for their lay counterparts. If the college faculty needed a Ph.D. in a given field, you might simply be plucked out of your normal routine and sent to graduate school full time, all expenses paid, to get whatever doctorate was needed. Just so had I myself left Mundelein in 1957 to study in the graduate school at Fordham. (Even the university was designated!) Fortunately I was teaching in a field I loved and the prospect of reading my way from Beowulf to Virginia Woolf delighted me. Four years later, as I finished up research for a dissertation on the music and poetry of eighteenth-century England, I had only one goal in mind — to get back to my college English classes for which at last I felt superbly equipped. Then came *my* letter. Would I please take on the job of academic dean instead? Sister Mary Donald was on the verge of retiring and running back to her loved Ovid and Homer. And since I now had my Ph.D. . . . So I had my long moment of anguish, tucked my dissertation in my trunk, and wrote back a reluctant yes. Thus, in the old dispensation, were deans created by higher superiors, without so much as a glance in the direction of faculty advice and consent.

The Modern Language Association and the College English Association were elbowed aside by the American Conference for Academic Deans, the American Association for Higher Education, the Association of American Colleges. Chaucer and Sam Johnson yielded to David Riesman and Nevitt Sanford. And, in a few months, back to school I went, this time to Harvard for a Carnegie-sponsored workshop for new deans. Over the next seven years as I viewed the college from an administrative point of view, how often I thanked my lucky stars for that brief internship where, along with thirty other neophyte deans, I tackled academic problems via the case-history method. By the time I left the job in 1968, I could have contributed a few spectacular case histories of my own.

During those years Mundelein followed up its institutional analysis by redesigning the liberal arts sequence and creating a continuing education program for an adult population of mature women. As dean, I learned the bitter truth of the old academic adage that changing a curriculum is like moving a cemetery. I emerged from that experience with lots of political know-how and a healthy respect for the survival instincts of department chairmen under siege. I'd been through the seven lean years of the deanship and felt more than ready for the seven fat ones. It was high time for a sabbatical, time for some retooling before a return to teaching. I knew I was setting a precedent when I entered the president's office to resign instead of asking my provincial for a transfer. But this was one of the happiest results of the Self Study — the professionalization of the religious faculty — and I wanted to dramatize the new status of the nuns at Mundelein. Totally in agreement, Sister Ann Ida concurred. So readily, in fact, that at a farewell luncheon I later admitted to the faculty that she had accepted my resignation with the same enthusiasm with which she had appointed me!

In September, then, I shook the dust of administration from my feet and headed for a post-doctoral fellowship in Yale's department of English. Then it was back to Emerson, Jonathan Edwards, D. H. Lawrence, and Thomas Mann. Presley McCoy, newly appointed chancellor of Johnston College at the University of Redlands, invited me to help plan the humanities program at that brand-new school, and for a few months I found myself commuting between New Haven and California. It was a halcyon interim before my return to classes at Mundelein the following September.

And there the story might have ended save for a telephone call one January day from Rudolf Waters, dean at Alcorn A&M and a confrere from the Harvard workshop. By the time our conversation had ended I had promised to help him find someone to teach English at Alcorn. And by the time March had rolled around, I knew very well I couldn't deliver.

But Dean Waters, never a man to be put off, suggested an alternative: "Why not come yourself? Think about it. Anyway [and he played his trump card] come to see us before you decide."

And so I went. Everyone in the house went. We rented a white Impala and drove down to see what we could see. There was, after all, no harm in looking. Pres McCoy had just made me an almost irresistible offer to join the Johnston College faculty. But while I was turning that one over in my mind, why not just look over the situation in Mississippi?

It's easy to see now with the omniscience of hindsight that the moment I crossed that cattle guard at the entrance to the Alcorn campus my decision was in effect already made. If ever a situation spoke mutely of need, it was this big, straggly, raw campus hidden away in the depths of Mississippi. Johnston College would have no trouble recruiting faculty; they were already standing in line. Alcorn was another kettle of fish. It didn't promise anything but challenge. But, Lord, it was big on that!

In one sense, Waters's offer couldn't have come at a better moment. In the congregation it was becoming clearer and clearer that the old way of assigning nuns to jobs was creaking to a standstill. The Council had urged us to respond to the needs of the world. For the most part, however, we were tied to the needs of the Church. Parochial school systems and hospitals swallowed up most of the nuns. Catholic high schools and colleges depended on the large pool of available talent. But among the nuns there was a mounting desire to break out of this closed mode of operating. BVM's wanted to retrain for parish ministry. They wanted to get into public school systems, particularly in the inner city where Catholics were a meager minority but where human problems were dense.

As long as the nuns had no voice in where they put their efforts, as long as mothers general and provincials alone dealt with diocesan school superintendents and made decisions as to where and how many nuns various regions of the country would get, the possibility of responding to new and urgent needs was practically nil. Somehow decisions had to be brought down to the level of the individual Sister.

All that spring, as I was going through the process of getting a leave of absence from Mundelein to go down south, discussion of the need to diversify the community apostolate was building to a climax. When the community senate met in California in August, one of the first items on its agenda was TOPA. It didn't pass easily. But it passed. And as the events of the next few years were to prove, endorsement of this new personnel policy began to accomplish the most spectacular about-face BVM life had yet seen.

What precisely was TOPA? A proposal that, far from being assigned, nuns should have the option of applying for whatever jobs they wanted. As a modus operandi for lives rooted in the tradition of obedience to a superior, this idea was nothing less than revolutionary. Theologically, it had significant implications for change, for it predicated a new concept of obedience, a new approach to poverty, to corporate responsibility, to community. And, added its proponents, it had implications as well for personal "response-ability," since it made each woman responsible for the choices affecting her destiny. In the eyes of its creators, TOPA was a kind of touchstone of renewal, a measure of just how serious we were about *aggiornamento*.

Certainly we were onto serious ground when we began to rethink the concept of obedience. From one point of view, obedience is the essence of religious life — the vow which encompasses the others, the only vow which some religious make. Vows are made to God. They are promises to do something pleasing to Him. The thrust of the vows is toward a total giving of oneself. In not marrying, one makes a gift of one's heart. In owning nothing, one makes a gift of one's individuality (things are extensions of oneself). In willing only what one's superior wills, one makes a gift of one's person.

In an older, simpler time novices were taught that obedience lay not only in the performing of another's will (which was for the religious the visible will of God) but in the interior acceptance of that will as being best for one. And perfect obedience lay in the identification of one's own will with the will of the superior. The ideal was prompt, generous, joyous obedience. Every BVM novice knew by heart the story of St. Ignatius who, at the sound of the bell, was said to have stayed his hand in the very formation of a letter. On July 31 of each year in all houses of the congregation, St. Ignatius's famous letter on obedience was read aloud. The injunction in that epistle was to unquestioning, loyal, and if possible "blind" obedience. The metaphor was military.

Paradoxically, the vows were meant to make us free, with the liberty of the children of God. And on one level at least indeed they did. Having neither kith nor kin, nuns had given no "hostages to Fortune." They traveled light. They had no lust for power, for authority. In short, down to the very last detail of our most intimate lives, our behavior was imposed on us by the choices of others. Intellectually, we knew that we were in reality free. Having freely placed ourselves in this state of unfreedom, we comforted ourselves with the illusion of freedom. ("I can split at any moment!")

Yet psychologically, the effects of this rigidly structured system were frequently disastrous. Until placed in positions of authority, nuns had practically no experience in decision making. As a result, they could often be quite helpless. (I recall one nun I lived with who, faced with the necessity of deciding whether or not to attend a theater party, finally seized a coin and tossed it. And this was a woman in her fifties who headed a college department of economics and gave the appearance of intelligence and maturity.) For the most part, nuns tended to be outer- rather than inner-directed, like the nun who confessed to me that she hated Sundays and holidays because she never knew what to do with herself. Since one always had to be ready to move on — today in New York, tomorrow in Montana — lives tended to be fragmented and personal relationships transitory. One was to be "a willing instrument in the hand of God," unconcerned as to the task He used one for. Few nuns were active in professional organizations. If elected to office, you might not be there to serve the following year. When at Mundelein the religious faculty voted to join the American Association of University Professors, it was thought sufficient to pay dues for only three or four people who could represent the rest of us.

A searing memory for me is the anger of a talented American Indian girl who had been my student in piano shortly after I began to teach. Over the summer, superiors decided that I should drop graduate study at Chicago Musical College and begin a master's degree program in English at Wisconsin. A shift in faculty assignments had left the college magazine without a sponsor and I was told to exchange my keyboard for a Smith-Corona. No Myra Hess, I was not exactly desolated by the order. To Lucille, however, my departure represented merely the latest in a series of personal broken treaties. My explanations must have struck her as cold and unfeeling, however theologically based. They could not erase the feeling of abandonment such an abrupt severing of a relationship had created in her. Watching her draw back, bewildered, hurt, cagey again, I knew that there was something dehumanizing in such detachment. I felt it keenly but at twenty-six I had no notion of how to deal with it. I had to shut a door on that aspect of my life and to open another. When I'd learned in the novitiate what obedience meant, no one had mentioned that I might have to close that door in the face of a stricken, tearless Indian girl who had grown to trust and to love me as her teacher.

It seems to me now that Lucille Bruner was right. She could not understand how one could simply shut the lid of a Steinway grand and put away the Schumann, the Brahms, the Bach on which one had been working five to six hours a day. She couldn't take in the abrupt transition from studio to editorial office, where talk of "first drafts" and "line drawings" replaced concern for cadenzas and turns. The hostility in those suddenly unfriendly black eyes is the sharpest memory I have of that abrupt transition in my life. It marred the serenity, the certainty which my compliant obedience should have given me. That certainty which in no way promised *success* in a totally new situation but merely assured me that it wouldn't *matter* if I didn't succeed. And it is this attitude which was perhaps the most damaging aspect of our earlier understanding of obedience.

Our novitiate training was clear: *if you were obedient, you could not fail.* If you were badly placed, if you were given unintelligent orders, someone else's bad judgment was at fault, not yours. Besides, if you did fall flat on your face in one assignment, you'd have another in a trice. In the community there was no such thing as being out of a job. It was an inside joke that that was how we got some notoriously bad superiors — by lateral promotion! We operated on the Peter Principle long before it reached the public press. "Perfect obedience" dissolved all possibilities of failure and its consequences in the "real world." It fastened its eyes on Heaven where it was certain that utter compliance did not go unnoticed. What damage such a concept did in terms of human productivity, how much natural talent and energy it smothered — these are incalculable. For every Gerard Manley Hopkins, singing unheard at his "day-labour" in Wales, for every de Chardin ferreting out life's mysteries in Chinese exile, a thousand lesser lights flamed briefly and died, the fresh draft of natural ambition cut off at the source.

Happily, by Vatican II, almost none of us still entertained so naïve a view of obedience, so static a concept of the will of God. It was becoming clear to us that obedience must be put into a larger context — that of compliance with the Gospel imperative. The notion of collegiality as explicated in the Council documents made this very clear. If the Church is the People of God, it is in them that authority is vested. Decision making should be a shared experience. As theologian Avery Dulles phrased it, the individual religious exercises his freedom by sharing in the group decision, then freely obeying it.* Translated out of theological jargon, this principle was enormously liberating. It shattered beyond repair the old model of military obedience which had dominated seminary and novitiate training. One's obedience was not to the explicit command of the superior (like that of a private to his lieutenant). It was to the law itself, the Gospel law which commands all of us to love our neighbor as ourselves.

TOPA was Sister Margaret Mary Whelan's inspired mechanism for achieving grass-roots involvement in decision making. It promised a marvelous freedom of choice. It provided a mode of discovering what the corporate thrust of the group really was. (Did we in fact wish to restrict ourselves to running traditional Catholic schools or were BVM's indeed reaching out to creative new minis-

---

* *Kinetics for Renewal*, ed. Sister Rita Benz and Sister Rosemary Sage (Dubuque, Iowa: Communication Center, 1969), p. 17.

tries?) The day was past when such decision for the group could effectively be made by one person or by a few at the top.

Yet it came as a shock to discover how unready for freedom so many of us were. Simone de Beauvoir has noted that Galen, an authoritarian second-century writer, was convinced of his own infallability because he wrote at a time "when people preferred belief to argument."* Clearly many among us would also choose belief over freedom, preferring unfreedom and the security of authority to the risk of choice — for at the BVM California senate of 1970 opposition to TOPA was intense.

A subliminal fear of anarchy permeated many of the arguments against the proposal. If everyone chose for herself, what would become of order, the power of authority, of "corporate responsibility"? Wasn't there a danger of hidden agendas? Might not people choose a situation in terms of their own self-fulfillment rather than in terms of community commitment? And there were other fears — that in tiny, remote parishes or places linked to "impossible" pastors or tyrannical superiors certain schools might simply have to close for want of nuns. Would even Sister Cunegunda (good soul) choose Jessup, Iowa, if she could get to Glendale, Chicago, or Long Island? An assistant superintendent of schools questioned the prudence of the timing: other religious congregations might be threatened by our "open" applications. We could imperil the viability of diocesan high schools now staffed on a quota basis by several different orders. (Among senators the word went out that, being a school superintendent, this speaker had a vested interest in the status quo. Her influence waned.)

Support for TOPA focused on response-ability — the capacity to respond to new and emerging needs. Margaret Mary Whelan had

---

* Simone de Beauvoir, *The Coming of Age* (New York: Putnam, 1972), p. 18.

dreamed up the concept in an attempt to free people from the traditional classroom for full-time involvement in religious education. Hers was a brilliant notion and, as it turned out, prophetic. There was, she sensed, a far wider field of endeavor opening up to nuns. But they would have to be trained in the new theology in order to serve on parish teams, to work with adults as well as with children. Alienated by changes in the Church which they could not understand, middle-class parents were pulling their children out of Catholic schools. ("How Catholic are classrooms that never see a nun anyway?") It might well be that the nun of the future would be found in the public schools — or working directly with the very poor, in ghettos, in areas where the congregation had not served before.

Already BVM's were moving into run-down apartments in Chicago's uptown district or on the West Side, just providing a "presence," just being available until they could sense the real needs of the very poor. In time the Sisters of Providence would outrage suburban Catholics on the North Shore by voluntarily closing Marywood Academy in order to keep open predominantly black Providence High School on the South Side. When there weren't enough nuns to go around, communities simply had to reevaluate their priorities. There were other schools for middle-class Catholic girls. There were, however, no options for the dispossessed minorities at the bottom of the ladder other than the junglelike public schools into which they jammed. That most of these students were not even Catholic was just salt in the wounds of shocked Catholic parents who angrily criticized the nuns for "abandoning" them.

The whole school issue was a thorny one and nuns lined up on both sides of the question. Catholic people had indeed sacrificed to build the largest and most impressive system of parochial schools in the country. If Chicago was predominantly a Catholic city, it was largely due to the nuns who had taught successive generations of children in that city since the Great Fire. The BVM's themselves had come to Holy Family parish in 1870 at the request of Father Arnold Damen, S.J. Now there existed a network of solidly built, well-furnished convents attached to shining, sturdy parochial schools. And the nuns wanted to move into ghetto apartments, into storefront schools? If nothing else, one had to think about all that property. TOPA could mean the death of the Catholic school system.

The central importance of Catholic education had been a major factor in my deciding to enter the congregation. But some of us now began to see ourselves as prisoners of our own past, trapped into maintaining institutions we ourselves had created. Once Authority had assigned us to schools, Someone else up there — a provincial, a mother general — made the decisions. Perfection lay in prompt and entire obedience. Now, however, decisions were to be made by the group: everyone shared in the forming of consensus, then gave obedience to the decisions they had helped make. The new obedience lay in responding to the needs of the world, to the movement of the Spirit, not to the orders of a superior.

If fewer nuns taught in parochial schools, this need not mean the end of the system. Lay teachers could bring a needed dimension to the school environment; curates with good educations and too little to do in the parish could at least handle religion classes. They taught in diocesan high schools. Why not in the grades? (Later, we made the galling discovery that what made nuns so attractive was that they cost so little. Often, when nuns left a school, the parish simply closed it. Obviously, Catholic education was not so essential as we had thought.)

In a real sense, the fight over TOPA was the central issue of the California senate in 1970. As debate continued, all the "code" words worked their way into the argument. To read the summaries of the senate sessions now is to see the emergence of the lexicon which birthed the changes of the sixties: collegiality, subsidiarity, personalism, corporate responsibility. Speaker after speaker admitted that TOPA was an idea whose time had come. It was implied in the guidelines for personalism and freedom adopted by the Tenth General Chapter of the previous year. We couldn't have the latter without the former. The needs of the Church, of a changing American society, differed from those of a nineteenth-century immigrant Catholicism. As Christians, we had to shoulder some of the problems of race and poverty and peace as well as the traditional school system. We must *really* give the nuns freedom to respond to perceived needs wherever these led. We must not so hedge in freedom that we neutralized the very possibility of risk. Sisters Margie Fieweger and Mary Cannon (still in their twenties, believers in "process" and eloquent advocates of change) urged the senate to give TOPA a chance as the best way of finding out whether or not it could work. Weren't we just assuming that California and Chicago would overflow with applications and the "dogs" go begging? (Two years later, California was indeed holding and Chicago couldn't fill well-advertised vacancies.) Maureen O'Brien boomed out her feeling that we were "waiting at the intersection of history while the light is flashing yellow." Amid laughter, she hoped that it would turn green, not red. Debate ended.

At a suggestion from the floor, Sister Roberta Kuhn, chairman of the senate and president of the congregation, telephoned Archbishop Flahiff to ask if we would have to poll the congregation to determine whether or not there was moral unanimity regarding open application. And would we have to apply to the Holy See for permission to allow to the Sisters the choice of their work? It was Solomon-like strategy. The Die-Hards could hardly reject the opinion of the Sacred Congregation for Religious (at which Flahiff represented American nuns). The Progressives welcomed the chance to send up a trial balloon to see how Rome stood on so sensitive an issue. It would be well to know what the traffic could bear before the senate adopted its resolutions. If Vatican II encouragement of collegiality and subsidiarity meant anything, it had to mean responsible decision making, a new emphasis on person. If bishops themselves were organizing into senates, priests into voluntary associations, lay people into diocesan councils, surely nuns should break out of the strictly hierarchical system which deployed them like troops, without a voice in their own destiny.

Archbishop Flahiff couched his position in the magic word "Experiment," the enabling euphemism through which change flowed freely into American religious congregations. The Vatican Council had given religious orders twelve years to experiment. Long before that period of grace expired, many of us could expect to have done so! We could try TOPA. We could, it turned out, try just about anything. Thus, just at about the moment when Twin Oaks was fleshing out Skinner's theoretical Walden II, the BVM senate, by a vote of 43 to 3, launched a social experiment of its own — one which, it appears, will permanently change the future for some American religious.

Certainly it changed my future. I signed and returned my contract to Alcorn A&M and arrived on campus in time for the faculty meeting in September, 1970. Out of habit, away from the community, I felt a bit like Chaucer's monk who "held thilke texte not worth an oyster" which told the monk he had no business out of cloister! Over the next three years, a minority group member on a totally black campus, I was to practice a new kind of obedience, of poverty.

I learned to what degree I was capable of response-ability. The theory and the code words came so easily. The experience itself was both utterly different from anything I'd known, and luckier. For me it worked. I knew the freedom of the children of God. I found it both sweet and frightening.

CHAPTER EIGHT

MISSISSIPPI JOURNAL

In the mainstream they talk about "digging it,"
about "getting it together" ! That's our speech,
man. How come?
— ELIAS BLAKE, JR.

The first time in my life I realized I was white was the day I pushed my way into the Alcorn College Union to pick up my mail. Outside, students lined the low brick wall leading to the entrance. They lounged in clusters that seemed all blue jeans and tank tops, punctuated here and there by a few Afros. I could sense their eyes on me as I passed. Not smiling, but not hostile either. Just watching. I felt uncomfortably conspicuous, like someone showing up for a party in a chiffon formal when everyone else is in denim pants. The thought flashed into my mind: maybe this is the way the isolated black student feels at Mundelein. Inside the too-small Union, the crunch was bargain-basement hectic. I had the impression of beards and broad-brimmed hats, of bright oranges and reds and tight, tight pants, of rich throaty voices and words I couldn't quite catch and white teeth in lots of grinning faces. And I thought, "My Lord, I even *feel* white."

Yet, driving south along Mississippi Highway 61 that August of

1970, I wasn't thinking primarily in terms of color. Because my heart was pure (hadn't I stood with Martin Luther King against Bull Connor's dogs at Montgomery?), I anticipated few problems of assimilation. It hadn't yet dawned on me how ill-equipped I was for the job. One week in the classroom would rock me with that realization. I was into a totally new situation without any techniques to deal with it, all my previous experience practically useless. It was the first sobering step toward what I eventually labeled "the conscientization of Mary G."

I had been warned to avoid the least scent of messianism ("Don't come in walking on the water!") and, anonymous in a pink cotton shirtwaist, I comforted myself that I wasn't even recognizable as a nun. No matter how my community viewed my sojourn in the South, the only "mission" Alcorn College expected of me was an academic one. I had been hired to teach English, to serve on the inevitable faculty committees, to help the college take a noticeable step up as it moved into its second hundred years. For the first time since I'd entered, the fact that I was a nun was immaterial. I was "Dr. Griffin" to colleagues and students on a campus punctilious about titles. When they said "Sister" at Alcorn, they didn't mean me!

Except for Ruth Brady, the big-hearted Dominican nun with whom I was to share a tiny duplex apartment on campus, everything about Mississippi was excitingly new. Ruth and I had met as graduate students at Fordham and eight years later had rented an apartment together in New Haven while Ruth was spreading her wings as an industrial research chemist and I was studying at Yale. When I arrived in Mississippi, Ruth had already put in a year at Alcorn as acting chairman of the chemistry department. And she was elated enough over gaining a housemate to offer a quick tour of New Orleans before Mary De Cock headed back north.

In the steaming Mississippi heat, Ruth's air-conditioned car was

a veritable oasis. We swept through lovely miles of Mississippi —
winding roads margined with kudzu and bearded live oaks (I knew
the Spanish moss was a parasitical killer but it was pretty in its own
gloomy way). Louisiana, with its Hardyesque swamp willows,
seemed desolate and grotesque, like a Hollywood set for *Tess of the
D'Urbervilles*. Then suddenly we were onto the twenty-six-mile span
of bridge across the Pontchartrain and heading for one of the
prettiest cities in the South.

In New Orleans we did the touristy things — the French Quarter,
dinner at Commander's Palace, café au lait at Port-of-Call. Then it
was time to start back, via the Gulf Coast this time, so we could
see the havoc Camille had wrought the previous year as she ripped
past Bay St. Louis, Gulfport, Pass Christian. The ghostly reminders
remained — freestanding gates, foundations stripped clean of the
houses they once supported, the roof and walls of an enormous
Georgian mansion totally innocent of an interior. Out in the Gulf of
Mexico a string of pier posts leaned away from the shore like a row
of decaying teeth.

Back at Alcorn, there is time only for a quick trip to Rodney, the
ghost town at the edge of the old dirt road which winds away from
campus. In the 1840's Rodney had been a flourishing river town
until one spring a demolishing flood erupted and the Mississippi
actually changed its course, leaving the town literally high and dry.
Today a little Presbyterian church clings crazily to its perch above
the road and long-abandoned shacks and tiny homesteads sink back
into the earth. We drive on to Port Gibson and pick up the
Natchez Trace Parkway which connects with Highway 20 leading
to the Jackson airport. When Mary's Chicago-bound Delta lifts into
the hot still sky, I feel that my last link with the North is really
broken. A faculty institute is next on the calendar. And we start the
ninety-mile drive back to campus so as not to miss it.

At the faculty institute I had a chance to get an overview of faculty and staff. Some 120 in all, they turned out to be surprisingly cosmopolitan. I spotted East Indians and Pakistanis, an unmistakably Arabic face, half a dozen whites (actually there were ten of us), and more women faculty members than I'd anticipated. Except for color, they reminded me marvelously of their counterparts at Mundelein — an early distant warning that campus cultures and campus politics don't differ appreciably. It was easy to pick out the "Old Guard" (impeccable with vest and watch chain and furled umbrella) and the "Young Turks" (bearded and long-haired, in faded pants, grayish T-shirts, striped tank tops), the traditionalists and the radicals. It was amusing being a newcomer and speculating on who was who, on what underlay those surface smiles and automatic phrases of welcome.

The main speaker of the faculty institute was Elias Blake, Jr., director of the Washington-based Institute for Services to Education. I listened with admiration as he swung easily from the jargon of academia to the lively metaphor of the Mississippi black. Dr. Blake addressed himself unapologetically to the newest arrivals on the faculty. "Don't be afraid to say 'I dunno' to students now and again. Otherwise, the student is always on *your* turf. You gotta be on *his* part of the time." He told us that the Thirteen-College-Study had discovered that 72 percent of black students in southern colleges come from families with less than a $3,000.00 income. The rest are in the $6,000.00 bracket — "the cashmere sweater set!" And, as he put it, 50 percent of them don't think they *can* learn. They begin college "with two strikes against them and a fast-ball pitcher on the mound." So if they've survived this far in a school system like Mississippi's and are trying to make it into college, the chances are that they're "bright, tough, and determined."

He urged the faculty to begin where the kids are — with *ideas*.

"Don't worry about the fact that they can't spell. Convince them that they *know* something. Maybe even enough to argue with *you!*" The important thing, according to Blake, was to open up to these students positive attitudes about learning. They must begin where they cannot fail. It was more important to tap their creativity than to correct their grammar. He was very funny about how he himself came to recognize the utter unreality of higher education when he was a student at Payne College in Georgia. He knew there was something phony about all those marble Greeks and Romans in the textbooks: they didn't look at all like the guy in Spiro's grocery! He urged us to get the kids reading what's around them — books by King and Malcolm X and Ellison and Cleaver — and then to hook into these with Socrates and Thoreau where they are relevant.

Blake pointed out that the black man has at times allowed himself to be exploited. Though he's in the minority, his patois has crept into American English. But he gets little credit for it. "How come," he asked, "how come the white man is talking about 'hangups' and about being 'strung out'? How come even the President of the United States can say, 'When the action is hot, cool the rhetoric?' *Cool it,* man! The President! In the mainstream they talk about 'digging it' about 'getting it together'! That's our speech, man. How come?" He explained the etymology of "hang up." Originally it was used by black jazz musicians who found themselves getting into difficult chord progressions without being able to get back to a resolution. They'd say they were "hung up." Then, said Blake, "the rest of the society 'grammatized' it and we got 'hang-up'!" Gershwin learned all about the "blue note" (not a minor, really in the crack) from James P. Johnson. He used to go up to Johnson's place day after day and try to figure out how he got that effect. Then he wrote "Rhapsody in Blue" (really "Rhapsody in Blues") and no one remembers Johnson. Benny Goodman learned it all from Fletcher

Henderson. Goodman made thousands and Henderson never made a cent. Yet jazz is *America's* music, not the black man's. "And we won't even let him into the mainstream!"

Blake's injunction in mind, I felt I had the situation well covered when I met my Junior Honors Seminar on the following Monday. There were eight top students, of whom seven were biology majors. (Of this group one would go to Johns Hopkins with a full scholarship in medicine; the rest would all make it into first-rate graduate schools.) To make sure that materials were available, I had had to select the seminar topic before the group met. I'd chosen to do a seminar in American minorities with a view to making these students aware that they were but one among many minorities in American culture. The more I myself had read, the more I was inclined to reject the "melting pot" theory in favor of ethnic and racial pluralism, what one journalist has called the "tossed salad" theory: most of us are green, some oilier than others, some a glossy black. But we fall together deliciously! In the course of the seminar we read Oscar Handlin's *The Uprooted,* Will Herberg's *Catholic, Protestant, Jew,* Nathan Glazer's *Beyond the Melting Pot,* Vann Woodward's *The Strange Career of Jim Crow.* And before we had got deep into any of these we took two weeks out to master Mortimer Adler's *How to Read a Book,* since even these very bright students had difficulty reading analytically and critically.

Week after week we parried, we stepped gingerly around each other. And week after week it grew increasingly evident that the most obvious minority among us was me — one of the handful of faculty people who kept Alcorn from being a totally black community. I was a Northerner in the South, an urbanite among students of predominantly rural backgrounds. Mine was a Catholic sensibility against a profoundly Protestant one. Finally, I was white and they were black — without exception. So it was inevitable that one day in seminar a student should ask me bluntly, "How does it feel to be a 'foreigner' on campus? What gets to you? How much of an outsider do you feel?" It was the beginning of free conversational exchange. I could almost hear the chains of constraint clattering to the floor around us. And that very day we launched our project: a study of attitudes among the minority nonblack faculty on campus — the "foreigners" as I that day discovered they called us all.

What we learned from that study I should have liked to share generally. But our methods I felt sure would not pass a rigorous inspection by the social scientists on campus. Someday they themselves may undertake such a study and it will be interesting to see how closely our findings coincide.

On the whole, the students saw the "foreigners" as valuable change agents: they brought to the college new ideas, new teaching techniques, a wider (at least, a different) experience, and (how happily I heard it) deep commitment to their students. The East Indians, the Asians generally, were sometimes hard for students to understand ("You too, Dr. Griffin. You talk so fa-ast!") and seemed to make very hard-nosed demands in their courses. But it was conceded that the outsiders had mastered their math, their chemistry, their biology, their political science. They were *good* teachers.

For their part, the foreigners openly admitted to the student researchers that they themselves felt largely excluded from the black academic community. They had rather expected the ostracism many of them experienced from the local white community. ("Well, no — I wouldn't advise you to apply for membership in the country club. It's not that we have anything against *you*, personally, you understand. But, well, you *do* teach at Alcorn and — ah — ") But it was indeed hard to sense that even on campus the nonblack faculty were being isolated socially, just left out or overlooked. One man who had been at Alcorn for a number of years was bitter about the no-man's-land he and his wife felt they lived in. "We give dinner parties, but — " His shrug was eloquent. "We are not asked to any."

Many of these people admitted frankly that they would leave Alcorn as soon as an opportunity turned up. They did not feel appreciated by the faculty generally. They had no voice, little hope of promotion, as yet no possibility of tenure. So they were afraid to speak out. They might lose their jobs and jobs were beginning to be hard to come by. Kynard Adams summed it up: "I think a lot of them stay here just for a job; I can't blame them!" Kynard's research showed that though white faculty members reported some hostility from students, they tended on the whole to find greater acceptance in the classroom than among their black colleagues. Yet they made a distinction: the younger the black faculty, the more open to "outsiders." The more established, the more distant. An enlightened administration was credited with bringing the "foreigners" to campus. But back of it all students sensed that there loomed the increasingly specific demands of HEW — the clear imlication that a flow of federal funds to the New South was directly related to the implementation of a policy of integration.

For all of us it proved a fascinating experience to translate the study of minorities out of the textbook and into our everyday lives. De Tocqueville had warned against the fatal weakness of the "tyranny of the majority"— that bête noire of democracy. In a minuscule way, the nonblack faculty had suggested to their student interviewers one form that tyranny can take — the form of exclusion, of isolation, of alienation. This was a new awareness for Mississippi blacks — to realize that, looked at from another perspective, they themselves came on as "the majority" — and not a flawless one at that! "It's who sits in the seats of power, man!" as someone summed up the seminar at its close. Privately, I savored the irony of it all. Part of the great white majority "out there," I came on to my students as one of a tiny, not-very-powerful minority at Alcorn. It's who sits in the seats of power indeed!

Of all the papers we worried out over a two-year period, however, the most unforgettable was the one Willie Adams wrote during the seminar on Tocqueville's *Democracy in America.* In 1835 the French writer had delineated the future America must expect unless it came to grips with the race question. Willie, a pre-med student, now looked to "The Future for Blacks in the Field of Medicine." For the seminar meeting he'd put on his best — a dark gray silk suit, matching shirt and tie, his fraternity emblem. Tall, "imperiously slim," he had the high cheek bones of his Indian and Negro background. One segment of that paper hit me hard. By the year 2000, Willie hoped to see blacks finally specializing in all aspects of medicine, not relegated to invisible tasks.

Negro physicians want to share with their white colleagues in all fields and not be limited to radiology, anesthesiology, and pathology. These limitations have been placed on the negro doctor in the past because in radiology the patient is in the dark and can't see the doctor; in anesthesiology he's asleep; in pathology he's dead — and it doesn't make any difference.

I can't forget that passage. Nor can I forget the quiet acceptance of its bitter irony by the rest of the seminar. It was always a puzzle to me: were my students really as emotionless as they appeared? Were they incapable of anger or just very skilled in repressing it? Or was their quiescence the result of a low level of vitality — the aftermath for many of inadequate nourishment during all their "Wonder" years? For some I concluded it was the result of a sort of glazed hopelessness about ever really making it up and out of

Mississippi. They were so *impassive* in class, even the brightest of them. But so delightful when occasionally their laughter erupted almost in spite of themselves. I felt guilty sitting in judgment on their responses, as if just by deciding how they ought to respond I was exercising another form of oppression.

The Honors Seminar had given me, I knew, the very brightest kids. My world literature course was something else. Alcorn hadn't yet dropped required courses and this one confronted me with forty-eight condemned prisoners. The first day the class met I sized up those impassive enduring countenances and silently prayed for a fire drill.

I had cased the enrollment beforehand and could classify on sight a few of the more prominent members. There sat Willie McGee, the fastest human in the world (he'd just set the world's record for the hundred-yard dash) and half a dozen other hulking football players of Green Bay Packer dimensions. When they trotted onto the field, they had to scare the opposition silly. But let me face them with a page of Sophocles' *Oedipus Rex* and, for the most part, they dwindled into mute, miserable boys. I closed the text, perched on the edge of the desk, and launched into a synopsis of that superb story in language as colloquial as I could make it.

A week later, as two or three talented readers did a book-in-hand presentation for the innocent rest of the class, excitement finally erupted and discussion took off: "Man, how could that cat Eddy-puss live with hisself? He had a thing for his own mammy and he done his old man in." We waded into *Antigone,* linking her across the centuries with Rosa Parks, Creon with George Wallace. Decades after the event, we admired audacious World War II French actors who had stiffened up the Resistance with a production of Anouilh's *Antigone* beneath unsuspicious Nazi noses.

Obviously there was a lot of untapped potential in my sophomores and it literally kept me awake nights devising ways to release it. But it was clear that my usual way of teaching literature simply would not work. For the most part these kids just hated to read; that was obvious. And the reason why was just as obvious: they were duds at it. When you shoot a consistent ten over par, you don't exactly yearn to get out on the course.

As McLuhan had suggested, my students were in a sense really pre-Guttenberg. Orally, they were enormously literate. Though they might fracture the King's English, come up with some creative spelling and some wonderful malapropisms, they also coined the freshest diction I had yet heard. They spoke their own patois, Black English, and it came on as a fresh and vigorous mode of communication.

No wonder that print didn't turn them on. All their lives they had focused not on the book but on the screen. This was the TV generation with a vengeance. Not words, dragging "their slow length along"— this was not their métier. But images racing past on a movie screen, or forming on a TV monitor as electronic impulses. That winter I read that Joseph Papp's *Much Ado About Nothing* was seen simultaneously by twenty million viewers — more people at a single performance than the combined audiences for every Shakespeare play ever produced. If Shakespeare were writing today, it probably wouldn't be in print. He'd be writing with light on film. What I needed was a private film series!

Enter Jane Trahey, New York advertising executive, who agreed to set up at Alcorn the Margaret Trahey Film Fund in memory of her mother, who she said made it to the movies at least three times a week. And suddenly we were in business, with the English faculty plowing through film catalogues instead of book lists.

The day *Othello* was shown the entire class showed up for the first time since registration. I'm not sure that we ever straightened out the maneuvers of the Turkish fleet off the coast of Cyprus or the precise location of Venice, but far past the class hour we debated the likelihood of some Natchez Desdemona's eloping with an Alcorn Othello from Claiborne County, Mississippi. Iago's anti-feminist speech to Desdemona crackled alive; Othello's "Put out the light and then put out the light" worked its chilling magic. And finally, how sweet the sound, "Hey, I dig this guy. What else did he write?" The resistance to reading poetry had been prodigious; the response to the film fantastic. And they had seen the play whole, not just a snippit of it. They had, at whatever distance, encountered the Renaissance world, not a mere garland of footnotes. I felt that I was on my way to solving World Lit. I. How much further could I push this freedom from the tyranny of the book?

Even as I asked myself that question, I winced at the heretical sound of it. Print was turning them off, however, and film was turning them on. Myself a book-aholic, I certainly did not wish to eliminate print entirely. There is no way fully to savor Iago's chauvinistic speech save by dissecting it, image by insulting image. There is no way to penetrate Othello's ironic metaphor except by unraveling the exquisite fabric of his language. Yet how much more readily students could be interested in Shakespeare's wordcraft once they'd grasped the play in toto. After seeing the play, they weren't so apt to be scared off by seventeenth-century diction and syntax. Obviously I had to start where my students were, to lead from their strongest, not their weakest, position, to start where the football team could plunge into discussion with the same assurance as could the few competent readers in the class.

Judging from the experience with *Othello,* there *was* a language they could handle at once and with ease — the language of film. If I could grab them there, where everyone was, in a sense, on equal footing, I might be able to lead them more willingly to the language of print. So the pattern emerged: from *visual* literacy to *verbal* literacy to *print* literacy. This was the revolutionary sequence we had to follow if we were not to move into the future with our eyes on the rear-view mirror. McLuhan had been saying it for ten years. But I hadn't really heard him until now when I needed to.

It worked with literature. Could it work with writing? Could I possibly create a learning environment in English I which would lead students freely to want what they were supposed to want in Freshman English — to learn to write?

I had not been assigned a freshman writing course that first year. But Vivian Tellis, who skillfully held the reins on a Hydra-headed humanities department, was delighted to give me a section to experiment with. The previous June I'd spent a couple of days looking at Paul Briand's multimedia writing program at New York State University in Oswego. What I saw was exciting: students turned on by 35 millimeter slide programs, responding to vivid impressions of controversial issues with on-the-spot writing that was fresh, spontaneous. Frequently they wrote on cassette tape and, for the first time in their lives, heard what they sound like. ("Shocks them to death!" said Paul.) Though he offered them, I couldn't borrow Briand's slide programs. To begin with, they were lily white. We'd have to make our own. But that meant getting cameras and film processing equipment, as well as tape recorders, overheads, transparency makers. It meant developing a program and getting it funded. All that spring and summer of my first year at Alcorn I worried out an experimental writing program.

"V-V-P: A Multi-Media Approach to English Composition" made the National Endowment for the Humanities' November 1 deadline by seconds. In late spring of 1972, NEH funded the program with close to $25,000.00. I asked for a third year's leave of absence from Mundelein and spent the summer working out course materials and ordering equipment. All the kids would have to supply were a number two pencil and blocks of yellow lined paper. Throwing out the traditional freshman reader and handbook, I sensed that as an English teacher I was deeper into heresy than ever. But always at my back I'd hear Blake's firm injunction drawing near: "They must begin where they cannot fail!"

So that fall I put an Instamatic camera into the hands of each of my students in English I and asked them to write not a verbal but a photographic essay. I wanted them to look hard at their century-old campus, their experimental farm, at their Afro'd fellow students, their multiracial teachers, at the surrounding if distant white communities, and eventually to put together photographic essays not only with unity, coherence, and emphasis, but with force and verve and style. I wanted them to structure their experience of reality through visual images, not written ones. (These — I counted on it — would come later and, hopefully, quite spontaneously.)

Malcolm X observed that every revolution starts with a change of mind. Ours started with a change of vocabulary. Suddenly our talk was of focus, balance, tension, texture. We discussed how pictures communicate feelings, make statements, suggest concepts. I had turned the initial third of the course over to Mel Hardin — a creative instructor in art — who made of it an exciting camera workshop (a significant investment of time in a sixteen-week semester). But long before the first film came back, we knew the course was working. In a school where attendance had just become optional, attendance in Mel's 8:00 A.M. photography class stood at 98 percent. Norman Pearson produced a sequence on "Love" memorable for its humor, its unselfconscious insights. Thomas Wyatt did a stunning photographic essay on "Alcorn as Ghetto," skillfully turning the eye of his camera first on the impressive new tower residence for men then under construction, next on the inescapable ugliness of much of the campus — the broken sidewalks, torn screens, ratty lawns, the slum look of even the newer dormitories with their narrow draperies yanked together and pinned any-which-way for privacy. Up in Jackson the city council had just thrown a twelve-foot-high chain-link fence across Lynch Street, the main artery of Jackson which bisects the Jackson State campus. The kids saw it as a new Berlin Wall. "Looks like a concentration camp up there!" Plans erupted to get the scene on film. One picture would be worth a thousand words.

Actually, this was my unspoken fear — that the language of film might seem so persuasive that they would see no need for words. (And this was, after all, a class in writing!) I knew that the day these kids made their first verbal responses to the student-made slides would be a crucial test. But after six weeks of shooting and viewing their own film, the strategy paid off. Students *wanted* to react to what they saw. They wanted to flesh out their documentaries with words and music. I need not have worried. They really wanted to get it all together. And they did so rather handily. They weren't a TV generation for nothing.

Mel and I had never spoken of "right" or "wrong": we never graded their pictures. We had talked about effectiveness: *effective* communication, *ineffective* communication. The pattern was set. Now we went right on using the same approach to our writing. Occasionally we took time out to note how misspellings or inept grammar blocked communication. But for the most part we concentrated on the writing process itself. Interest heightened as strikingly good pieces now and then emerged among the randomly chosen paragraphs flashed on the overhead. At semester's end (though a lot of mechanical weaknesses remained to be dealt with) no one came anywhere near failure. If not better than, their work was certainly as good as that turned out in any of the conventionally organized courses. And they had apparently lost their fear of writing. A tiny step, but a significant one toward the psychological freedom I feel that education is largely about. In addition they had been exposed to a whole new range of interests: the world of visual images. And they'd picked up a new vocabulary to discuss these.

Extending the range of freedom for my students by opening up to them their own untapped resources for the creation of and enjoyment of literature — that, I felt, was what my stay at Alcorn was all about. That my own sense of freedom was vastly expanding in the process was inevitable: any teaching relationship is dialogical. Either the teacher and the taught grow together or they both die a little in the process.

Doing this stint in the Deep South was probably a lot like being in the Peace Corps. Except for a prestigious handful of colleges like Fiske, Dillard, Howard, the Atlanta complex, black colleges have a rough time of it. Underfinanced, unevenly staffed, their students ill-prepared for advanced study, frequently remote from urban stimulation and opportunities, such schools have, as Alcorn's energetic president Walter Washington puts it, a "lot of catching up to do." Persuasive, eloquent, he managed in his first year of office to convince the Mississippi legislature that Alcorn A&M needed seventeen million dollars in "catch-up" funds just to begin to bring its pretty but neglected campus into shape. One thinks of Mississippi's traditionally white state schools — Ole Miss, Southern Mississippi — with their exquisitely manicured enclosed campuses, bright new buildings, up-to-date science labs, posh "Fraternity Rows" — nonverbal symbols of what Alcorn, Jackson State, raw young Mississippi Valley "might could be."

Students get around now. I took my Faulkner Seminar to browse in the Faulkner library at Ole Miss my last spring down there. They were probably too young to remember that only the National Guard could get James Meredith onto that campus less than ten years before. They took it for granted that black visitors might roam at will over those spacious greens. And they were right, as our welcome proved. Yet, thinking of how Paulo Friere's Brazilian peasants had reacted to juxtaposed pictures of their own squalid huts and the imposing homes of their overseers, I counted on my students mentally setting side by side images of Alcorn and of Ole Miss and asking themselves, "Why?"

Life at Alcorn, as on any college campus, was of course many-tiered. Tucked away deep in the heart of green, green country, fourteen miles from the nearest supermarket in Port Gibson or Fayette, we were almost monastically isolated. Twenty-six hundred students, some two hundred faculty and staff people, husbands, wives, children, cats, dogs — cheek by jowl we formed a community willy-nilly. Father Dominic Cangemi celebrated his carefully orchestrated liturgy, preached his exquisitely prepared sermons to the handful of Catholics who crowded the Newman trailer on Sunday mornings. But most of his student parishioners were not Catholic: they came for the color, the ceremony, the singing, which was loud and kind of late-nineteenth-century Protestant in flavor. It is their voices I hear in retrospect, blending in the painfully sweet final chorus which touched me as no Gregorian chant ever has.

> *O Lord, my God, when I in awesome won-der*
> *Consider all the works thy hands have made,*
> *I see the stars, I hear the roaring thunder*
> *Your power throughout the u-ni-verse displayed.*
> *Then sings my soul, my Savior God to Thee:*

How great Thou art — how great Thou art.
Then sings my soul, my Savior God to Thee:
How great Thou art —
How great Thou art.

If, initially, the blacks seemed distantly formal (at the first faculty friendship smorgasbord tiny islands of "foreigners" bobbled about in a dark cohesive sea), I came to see that this was essentially small-town wariness. Committee work eventually breaks through all barriers (the Tenure Committee forever cemented Claude Tellis and me!); the inevitable faculty-administration cleavage unites the most dissident elements even across color lines; Coach Cassem's Braves packed the cheering lot of us into the college stadium to see Jackson State or Tennessee Southern soundly trounced. When Dave Washington was drafted by the Denver Broncos; when Margarett Bachus was accepted into Meharry Medical School; when Dr. Morris announced a $400,000.00 grant for agricultural research, when the white board of trustees tapped Ernest Boykins, our popular arts and science dean, to be president of Mississippi Valley State at Ita Bena —community pride was tangible. If Alcorn people were somewhat inbred, there was plenty of reason for it. Except for a little bar halfway down the Seven Mile Road, there was really no place to go. So when Clarence Carter Smith took over the baby grand and gave us a night of song, when Jim Rayfield produced *Ceremonies in Dark Old Men,* when the mixed choir sang, or Alcorn's marching band stepped out at Homecoming, all of us were there. Laughter too wove its imperceptible web and for that time at least isolation vanished.

I think of the Boldens' farewell brunch, the little house crowded by a many-hued potpourri of faculty, staff, administrators, and everyone breaking up at stories about college days at Xavier in New

Orleans. *There,* I was admonished, nuns were *nuns* with habits and veils and rosaries in hand (not gin and tonic!). And the nuns got them to chapel, and got them to Mass, and flashlight in hand got them out of the shadows after late-night dances!

Through all the banter that afternoon there ran an undercurrent of nostalgia. We all felt it — the almost tangible regret for the lost world of cloister, of nuns "breathless with adoration," of veil and mystery, of naïve innocence and visible goodness. But the moment was ephemeral, for these are but the local color of religious life. They do not touch the center which has to do with the fullness of Christianity — with sharing the Good News, with redeeming time. No one really wants to go back.

TOPA had freed me to choose to go south. I had told Dean Waters, "A year then . . ." and I had stayed three. Now I found it hard to leave. I had thought of myself as giving. In reality I was on the taking end. I had had so much to come to terms with — my own insecurity, the limitations of my past experience, my largely ineffectual pedagogical baggage, my whiteness. Winding up affairs in Mississippi made me realize what it means to be accepted by the community one lives in. How one has to *earn* it when it doesn't come as birthright by virtue of creed or dedication or habit. My kids still couldn't punctuate (some marks of oppression are perhaps finally ineradicable), but I have a feeling Elias Blake might hand me a passing grade. Still — this was an ambiguous chapter in my life. It defies a neat summing up. I guess I'm still too close to it.

CHAPTER NINE

THE ETHIC OF CHASTITY

> ... *What distinguishes American writing is*
> *exactly the fact that we are strangers to each*
> *other and that each writer describes his own*
> *world to strangers living in the same land with*
> *himself.*
> — ALFRED KAZIN

"Sexuality" could have had only a pejorative connotation in my novitiate. We rarely heard the word *body,* let alone so obscene a word as *sex.* It was, to borrow Rosemary Ruether's graphic metaphor, "the beast in the belly."* One's body was "the unbecoming self" to be chastized into subjection so that the higher self, one's soul, might soar. Novices inhabited a classically dualistic world of body-soul discontinuities. Cultivation of the latter preoccupied our days and our nights. As for the former, the less said, the better.

Both the language of our Rule and the mind-set of our Novice Mistress were decidedly Platonic. Novices she perceived as pure angelic souls, somewhat unfortunately (if not misguidedly) lodged in the bonehouse of the body. But this latter was to be treated as a rag of no consequence — one destined for the dung heap in any

---

* Rosemary Reuther, "The Becoming of Woman in Church and Society," *Cross Currents,* Fall, 1967, p. 418.

event. Only when the body couldn't be dragged or driven another inch was one to yield to its importunities — and then with no good grace. It was washed in furtive haste (the huge drafty bathrooms all glowed eerily with ten-watt bulbs), fed plain food in silence, begrudged a scant seven hours of sleep in torrid or freezing zones, made to shiver away the winter in flimsy serge cloaks, swathed in armorlike layers of knitted underwear and striped petticoats, suffered to sit on only the hardest of straight-backed chairs, sentenced to kneel endlessly on unpadded benches, never affectionately hugged by another, and never, *never* looked at.

One of my earliest surprises was the discovery that there was not a single mirror in the novitiate. Since our handbags had been whisked away on the night of our arrival, along with all such worldly vanities as tweezers and compacts, the more imperfect among the postulants were reduced to glancing surreptitiously into the glassed doors of schoolroom book cases which dimly reflected our scrubbed, glossy faces, innocent of cosmetics.

Peering through a felicitous opening in my dormitory alcove curtains, I discovered, however, that novices were permitted the use of a tiny mirror by which to "pin" themselves into the intricacies of their headdresses. At dawn the first morning in the convent, I flattened myself against my pillow and watched Sister Claudia get dressed. If those intent black eyes met my own wide-staring ones, I knew I'd expire with shame, a "voyeur" in the novitiate! But this was serious business for Claudia; every moment counted if she were to make it to the chapel on time. Scarcely breathing, I hung on each skillful movement.

Under the folds of an enormous long-sleeved nightgown, she armed herself. First, those awful black cotton stockings — green from a year's novitiate laundering. Knit drawers and long-sleeved shirt. ("Dear God — hideoso!") Then the ankle-length petticoat, its knee-level pocket bulging with the huge men's handkerchiefs nuns used, the habit, the apron, and — oh, mystery of mysteries — the headdress. Claudia zipped a little mirror out of her commode drawer and snapped it onto the splasher. The sun was higher now and its first pink rays caught her head like a spotlight. She reached for her nightcap, and, sick with apprehension, I squeezed my eyes shut. If she were bald — vocation or no vocation — I was leaving on the noon Zephyr. But that fine thin face was framed with short-cropped hair so black it glinted blue. She was actually rather good-looking in a boyish way. And — delicious — she knew it too! The admiring glance died aborning, however. The 5:20 bell rang. Long lean fingers veritably threw on the border, yanked it into place, seized the veil, and reached for the curtain rings separating our alcoves. I was a dead woman as Claudia hesitated an awful moment beside me. Then the door opening and closing, the sound of heels tapping toward the stairs. And the strangled breath broke from my lungs. The Lord of Abraham, Isaac, and Jacob be praised: they weren't going to shave our heads. That nun in *Anthony Adverse* was just a piece of Gothic fiction after all!

In retrospect, it seems to me now that the religious habit was designed not merely to conceal one's person from the world, but from oneself as well. From the Fathers of the Church on, Christian tradition viewed woman as the cause of all man's woe. And nuns, it appeared, had totally internalized this self-image, hiding their femininity in yards and yards of fine black wool. One's hair was veiled, one's arms encased in multiple sleeves, one's bosom flattened under scapular or cape. Neither male nor female, nuns constituted a kind of neuter third sex.* Even so, the Rule warned, "Never for the shortest space of time shall they [the Sisters] be alone with a man,

---

* Marquette University housing application forms for summer session at one time asked students to indicate: Male_____, Female_____, Religious_____.

unless the door be open." Looking over the novices, it is inconceivable that one of us could have vamped the iceman. Nevertheless, preparing for vows of poverty, chastity, and obedience, we took such admonitions seriously, leaving the parlor door ajar as fathers and brothers squirmed through endless visiting Sundays.

Swathed in serge and linen, my sensible black oxfords anchoring me firmly where I stood, I felt myself no femme fatale, that's certain. But memory was traitorous. And, at a distance, even the clods I'd eluded at college tea dances seemed madly fascinating. My will might be dauntless, but my heart now and then, during an excruciatingly long Holy Hour, might long just a bit after fleshpots I'd forsaken in Chicago. So it was wise to chop off one's hair and to fasten the cloister door firmly behind one's weakness. Within those walls we had God. And we had each other. To a point. In the novitiate we were to discover that friendship — if "particular" — was considered a distinct nonvalue.

Ever on the lips of our Novice Mistress was the word "love." But this, we came to see, was "love" of a peculiar, nonpersonal, certainly nondemonstrative character. Novices were expected to be "general." They were to love everyone, but no one in particular. To love the genus, I told myself wryly, not the species! The Rule affirmed this position: "particular friendships" (exclusive attachments) were to be avoided, since in a very short time "these could overthrow the entire community." If Sister Mary Majella was surprised at the looks of confusion and disbelief on the faces of her new novices to whom such a concept of friendship appeared just this side of insanity, she betrayed nothing. Instead, she hedged us round with behavioral regulations. Novices were never to sit twice by the same person at recreation. They never took walks in twos but always at least in threes. No one might help out a fellow novice with a task nor lend her so much as a needle without permission. Never under any circumstances were novices to speak to one another in the dormitory. And if they broke the Solemn Silence they must report this infraction before breakfast in the morning.

Shades of total institution closed about the neophyte. In a life already regimented from dawn to dusk, such regulations filled in even the tiny crevices one hoped might have been missed. The "Perfect Novices" walked the prescribed chalk line — eyes habitually averted, lips sealed outside of recreation. You had to admire this metamorphosis, for it was some of the more blithe spirits among us who thus sternly took themselves by the scruff of their religious necks. But there were times when you could cheerfully have strangled those stiff necks too. Times when, dashing up the back stairs sweaty from "dishes" (with two hundred novices the task was gargantuan), one groaned at the sudden recollection that one had utterly forgotten the freshly starched headdress left to dry behind the kitchen stove and by now burned to a rich chocolate brown. It wasn't to the Perfect Novice you would then creep after lights out. It was to some "good Joe" like yourself who would slip you a fresh one without a question and conveniently forget the ruptured silence. In the innocent underground of novitiate, friends did find each other, illegitimate laughter did bubble behind ferns, over steaming laundry tubs, in illicit birthday cards, over contraband fudge or freshly baked rolls gulped down in the attic with only a shocked mouse to observe. But God help the novice inept enough to get caught. In the closed world of the novitiate, punishment could be swift and cruel. Examples were made. And for a long time afterward even the most daring conformed utterly.

Kathy was the first victim I witnessed. It wasn't friendship that proved her undoing. Kathy had no warm inclinations toward the rest of us. A Canadian, edging thirty, she kept herself aloof from our lapses into adolescent horseplay, spent every moment she could garner in one of the tiny piano rooms, practicing five-finger exercises or racing the "Ritual Fire Dance" to death. Kathy was a cold fish, albeit a pious one. Her crime was not one of human warmth. It was vanity: she shaped her hood too flat on top.

In the matter of habits, novices constituted a living footnote to Erving Goffman's *Asylums*. As college girls, we had worn our hair to the shoulder, scuffed up our saddle shoes in the expected manner, twitched out short pleated skirts in identical rhythms, and never glanced at how the nuns dressed. They wore habits; they wore veils; they looked gruesome. So what else was new? Once in the stratosphere of the novitiate, however, we assimilated to esoteric dress with horrifying alacrity. On the day of Reception the scales dropped from our eyes. There was, we realized, an infinite range of talent in that world of conventual fashion. Sharp-looking novices wore narrow pleats that flowed around them with alarming grace. Their borders framed their young faces in becoming lines; the stiffly starched hoods to which they attached their snowy veils were straight with rounded corners. Peering out of our new headdresses like great overgrown babies in bonnets, we despaired of ever mastering the art of "quilling" a border, of "shaping" a hood. Skills that wouldn't have brought a dime out there in the "real" world here were the coin of the realm. A good quiller could barter her way through the maze of novitiate life like a guide in a Turkish sook.

And here Kathy's athletic fingers paid off. She could quill like a dream — and did, for herself alone. She learned early how to shape and flatten her hood. And she did this with such ease that she foolishly shrugged off the incessant admonishment of the Mistress that hoods must be *rounded*. Many a hapless well-turned-out novice was snatched into Sister Mary Majella's office, only to emerge with flaming cheeks and a sagging hood. But Kathy went buoyantly free, her borders finely quilled, her hood ridiculously flatter and flatter.

The day the ax fell was a cobalt-blue Saturday in April. It was suddenly hiking weather and the novices were bundled into sweaters and scarves and sent off through the woods to find the grave of Julian Dubuque. Three hours later, when I dashed to the dormitory floor to retrieve my cincture, I discovered The Horror.

Seated on a straight-backed chair in the doorway of St. Peter's dormitory squarely at the top of the great center stairs was Kathy, her back to the hallway. Except for her veil, she was fully clothed in her habit. Her serge skirts swirled about her, her cape fell demurely to her waist. But on her head perched that crazy flat hood revealing from the exposed back the intricate system of pins and strings by which Kathy kept it all together. Clumps of her straight black hair sprouted out of gaps and spilled untidily over her collar. And the hood — that horror of a hood — sat naked to public gaze, plastered with forbidden strips of heavy brown paper which accounted for everything: its geometric shape, its water-resistance, its infuriation of the Novice Mistress.

For three days Kathy sat in the stocks, sent to Coventry in the cruelest possible manner. Her tray-served meals came back untouched. Without a book, without a moment's distraction, her fingers clutching each other in white-knuckled fury, she sat staring at the uncurtained windows. The second day I crept upstairs and mercifully pushed the door shut. Half an hour later, it stood wide open again. (An informer in our midst.) On the third day Kathy left. As usual no word was spoken concerning her going. She was missing from the dormitory. Her Office book disappeared from the chapel. Her number was removed from the laundry list. The Wurlitzer upright was still. The Novice Mistress let it leak to one favorite or another that the punishment had fit the crime. For a week novice veils grew conspicuously rounder. And the case was closed.

But if "pride cum vanity" was a heinous crime, exclusive friendship among the novices was worse. Fortunately, however, the
chances of cover-up were better than with the habit. The matter was
more subtle and detection more difficult. "P.F.'s" were covered and
recovered in novice instructions, always so delicately and obtusely
that confusion was compounded. What was so wrong about friends?
The Novice Mistress herself had friends, one indeed that she
eulogized to the point of utter boredom. But hers were "holy"
friendships. One had the notion that such friends prayed a lot
together and spoke unendingly of God. I too had a friend — for
whom I thanked God a lot. But the rare moments we managed to
spend together were squandered on laughter and an occasional glass
of smuggled port. This was my Postulant Mistress. So I knew I had to
live a hidden life and grow adept at doubling back on my tracks,
skipping evening study hours, even ditching the Saturday afternoon
hike and walking in the opposite direction for a blissfully free hour
as I unburdened the miseries of the novitiate to this warm, amusing,
healthy human being who obviously needed me as much as I needed
her. Not because Providence protected us — my slightly guilty
conscience could not stretch that far — just because we were adept,
this exclusive friendship missed official comment if not observation.
(It may have helped to make friends with the Palace Guard.)

Others were not so lucky. On the Sunday afternoon walk to the
cemetery, as clumps of novices sauntered along, some always walking backwards as they clung to the fringes of the group, I spied with
amazement two senior novices strolling along, arm-in-arm. I knew
them both, liked them both, knew they were close. But this was
suicidal. The stream of novices flowed around them, reformed on
the far side without a backward glance. Finally when we caught up
and passed them, I did look back and, like Lot's wife, instantly
regretted it as I caught a glimpse of flaming cheeks and swollen

eyes. Good God: another fitting punishment. I had hit it. If these two preferred each other's company, they were going to have it officially — a week of it, together at table, together in chapel, together on duty, together at recreation. To give the novices credit, they loyally carried on as if they saw nothing at all. But the warning was a dramatic one. And no one missed the import. Good friends avoided each other like the plague for a while (I never missed a study period); there was a great deal of manufactured general joy in the novitiate. And, for me, at least, the last remote possibility of rapprochement with my Novice Mistress evaporated.

In an article on "Nuns in the World," written for *Commonweal* magazine in 1963, Michael Novak accused American nuns of living a life remote from his own. "American sisters sometimes convey an ethereal impression," he said. They seem like "women trying hard to live as though they were 'spiritual creatures,' as though they didn't need affection and were 'above' sex. One might think of American nuns as ladies, hardly as women. They do not seem to be of earth, and the general impression they give is perhaps rather Jansenist than Christian; their chastity seems negative and unreal, rather than passionate and alive."* To Novak most nuns conveyed an aura of sustained adolescence.

No one had yet assessed nuns so perceptively and I wrote to the editors of *Commonweal* to underscore my agreement with much that Novak had said. Though limited in some of his perceptions, he had unerringly found out the principal weakness in novitiate formation. It really was preoccupied with turning out "ladies," not women.

Certainly in my novitiate, back in the thirties, one did not speak to "ladies" of anything so gross as homosexuality. Yet that, no doubt, was the reality which lay beneath fears of particular friendship.

* Michael Novak, "Nuns in the World," *Commonweal*, November 29, 1963, 79:276.

With hindsight, I must admit that there were a few relationships I'd now tend so to characterize. But they were rare indeed, and should have been dealt with honestly and humanely. Lacking candor, religious life raised up the specter of "particular friendship" and for some unfortunate women placed all friendship strictly out of bounds for the rest of their lives. What painful isolation, what warping of personality this led to I saw clearly in the lives of certain nuns who had taught me in college and with whom I later lived. Incapable of friendship themselves, they viewed all associations among younger nuns with bitter and suspicious eyes. Dying, a Sister I had deeply admired admitted to me, "I have denied myself all human warmth and affection. And now it is too late."

The horror of religious life was not, I realized sadly, what its detractors, writing in the tradition of Maria Monk or *The Devils of Loudon,* took to be the dark underside of the convent. It was the emptiness, the hollowness of a life devoid of human love — however dedicated to God.

There is no question of the fact that homosexuality emerges as a phenomenon in any sexually monolithic society, and is a common problem in total institutions. When an American monastic religious order invited me to serve as a consultant to the self-study it conducted in the sixties, their professionally drawn-up questionnaire merely assumed the possibility of such a problem and asked respondents for frank responses to direct questions. Among religious congregations of women, however, such openness is rare. Even our own self-study of 1966 sidestepped a frontal approach and came at the matter obliquely with a question employing the euphemistic language of "particular friendship."

"Their chastity seems negative and unreal," Novak had written, "rather than passionate and alive." Undoubtedly this resulted largely from the way in which the vow of chastity was understood —

namely, not as a dynamic union with Christ, but as the discipline of celibacy. At least this was true for BVM's as I knew them. Whatever the language of the Psalmist — "Come, my love, my dove / My beautiful one in the cleft of the rock" — whatever the connubial imagery to which they were clothed in the habit — "Come, spouse of Christ" — the practical implication of the vow was simply a promise not to marry. And that, not because of a passionate attachment to Christ which precluded any such human relationship, but for the sake of the Kingdom. To remain single-minded, to be free to give all one's energies to the work of the Church, to live a simple poor life in common into which the responsibilities of wife and mother could not be intruded: this was the thrust of the vow of chastity as perceived among "active" religious, dedicated to works of service. And as if to underscore this attitude of mind, my own congregation deliberately rejected the symbolism of "Bride of Christ" somewhat incongruously practiced by other American groups. At Reception time, we wore a simple communion veil, very like that we had worn as children for First Holy Communion. There were no wedding dress, no wedding veil, no ring. Indeed, our Novice Mistress implied that such overt symbols bordered on the sentimental. And in this instance I tended to agree with her.

In all our preparation for the taking of vows, motivation was couched in very practical terms: service, availability, economy. Celibacy was a function of being a religious, not a state embraced for its own sake. Shortly before Profession, Sister Mary Majella made available to the novices a small collection of books ordinarily kept in her private reserve. I remember best two or three by Dom Columba Marmion: *Sponsa Verbi,* the virgin consecrated to Christ, *Christ, the Life of the Soul, Christ the Ideal of the Monk.* I suppose that most of us, if not all, at least glanced through this handful of books set aside for Profession novices only. Readings like these, however, always made me slightly uneasy, as if there were a dimension of religious life still light-years beyond me, even after two years of novitiate, even on the verge of taking vows. In much the same way, I discovered later, active religious tended as a class to feel themselves less holy than contemplative nuns. These latter were the real thing. And every once in a while, as if ascending the mountain of God, a BVM attempted to move into that cloistered world, entering the Poor Clares, the Carmelites. It was like a vocation within a vocation. But it was one to which I had no pretensions whatsoever.

I tried when I was a novice. I really did. I carried *The Ascent of Mount Carmel* to Holy Hour after Holy Hour. But I ended up reading so avidly, so delighted with St. John of the Cross's imagery, that I forgot all about launching out into meditation. Descriptions of physical intimacy with the Beloved, though I knew them to be metaphorical, at first embarrassed me, then distracted me into fantasies more Joycean than Johannine. I gave up on the mystics.

Then I tried heroic measures — I took "extra" adoration. (The normal routine already kept us at prayer and spiritual reading about three and a half hours a day). I could (and did) sit for hours before the Blessed Sacrament; I could encapsulate myself within the deepest silence and fold myself into an attitude of prayer after Holy Communion. But I *never* had a "felt experience of grace." Usually I couldn't even manage to stay awake! I realized finally that I was as unregenerate as ever Emily Dickinson had felt herself to be. The best I could hope for was to live the Rule as generously as possible in the interest of spreading the Good News through Christian education. I had not a single doubt about the perfection of the Catholic vision of life: it was absolute. I was as unswerving in my belief as any Puritan pilgrim aboard the *Arbella*. And I felt every bit as chosen under the Grand Design of Providence. To me the grace of vocation was irresistible. If for this I had to give up marriage (or at least the chance of it) so as to be free for assignment any-time, anyplace — well, so be it. On a natural level, I hated the very idea. On a supernatural level, I knew that God's grace would be sufficient. It wasn't, I told myself, exactly the end of the world.

But it was, marvelously (though until Betty Friedan I never adverted to it), a step toward the liberation of nuns. Especially for those of us who happened to escape the parish school syndrome where nuns, though lacking husbands, often found themselves patronized by fatherly pastors who felt it their duty to direct the lives of the Sisters in every choice from refrigerators to voting pat-terns. I recall a Sunday evening in the sixties at a parish convent on Long Island where I was spending a weekend's vacation from research in the New York Public Library. Without warning, just as a lively conversation was erupting after dinner, the pastor arrived, flanked by his aging maiden sisters, and bearing an ice-cream treat for the nuns. ("Oh, thaaaaank you, Father!") After the usual inanities, as faces froze into resignation, Father revealed the real pur-pose of his visit. Elections were coming up and he'd brought the full slate of Republican candidates to review for the guidance of his unworldly flock. That two or three of the nuns in that house were some of the sharpest political cats around and avid Demo-crats to boot only added a lagniappe to an otherwise unbearably condescending episode. We were too much "ladies" at that point to bare our political claws. This was, however, the dying vestige of an archaic sacerdotal caste system from which it once appeared that nuns had as little chance to escape as had an untouchable. Though there is still room for consciousness-raising sessions among nuns, most are among the freest spirits I know. Having cheated Fortune of the hostages of husband and family, many of them are as little male-dominated as any group of women in history.

Among nuns there is no tradition of dressing for men, competing for men, effacing themselves intellectually or professionally to male colleagues. Active nuns have long had full-time careers — administering hospitals, running schools, nursing homes, orphanages. They pioneered in women's colleges, served as presidents of these institutions, invaded all the male preserves in higher education. They rode, if they must, the "Ladies' Elevator" at the Union League Club but they showed up for the dinner meeting when called. Even throughout the massive post–Vatican II changes, papal institutes of nuns (responsible directly to Rome and not to the local Bishop) have for the most part enjoyed an autonomy and dignity which have left them singularly free. (The Immaculate Heart nuns of Los Angeles and the Glenmary Sisters of Ohio, both forced out of canonical status by intransigent bishops, stand as regrettable exceptions.) American nuns were born female, but saw marriage and children as only one of three possible options, not (as a leader of NOW puts it) as "manifest destiny." God's irresistible grace called them to complete another design with their lives. Though unforeseen, the result has happily been some 100,000 women ripe for the philosophy of liberation.

Like their sisters under the skin, nuns are developing a radically new self-image. And that image is largely conditioned by changing attitudes toward the vow of chastity. It is not without significance, for example, that the BVM senate of 1973, refining its statement of goals, refers not to chastity but to a promise of celibacy.

Canon law describes the religious state as one defined by public vows of poverty, chastity, and obedience — the three marks Catholics are accustomed to find in monks and nuns. In addition, the life traditionally exhibits a degree of withdrawal or cloister, patently designed to wall out the world to a degree consonant with the apostolic lives of religious. Operationally, however, it is primarily celibacy which the Church has made the sine qua non of religious life, as well as an absolute condition for ordination in the Roman rite. I can think of flagrant violations of the vows of poverty and obedience I have observed over the years in my own and other congregations. I do not recall one of these occasioning forced dispensation.

Yet, when Father Philip Berrigan and Sister Elizabeth McAlister announced in June of 1973 that they had been secretly married for the previous four years, Sister Elizabeth's congregation immediately presented her with a dispensation from her vows. This, despite the fact that she herself did not wish the dispensation and had not requested it. When Father Berrigan refused to ask for laicization (which would free him from his promise of celibacy as well as prohibit him from exercising his priesthood), he was automatically excommunicated from the Church. Both the Religious of the Sacred Heart of Mary and the Josephite Fathers were acceding to the canon of the Church which prescribes celibacy for religious. How long this unique relationship might have continued without the principals being expelled from their communities had the matter been kept private is a matter of interesting speculation. But once the news broke, there was obviously fear of scandal and ecclesiastical reaction was swift.

Recognizing that, as a result of their indictment and trial for conspiracy against the government, both were in a sense really public persons, Father Berrigan and his wife released a carefully worded statement to the press. It explained their views of religious life and rationalized their attempt to bring radical change to that state. Their lives, they said, had "converged in community and non-violent resistance, particularly to our country's warmaking in Indochina." For them religious life was defined by "community and non-violent resistance." "The Church," they wrote, "has made celibacy the spirit of religious commitment, if not the heart."

We had hoped that a time would come when religious communities would invite both celibate and married people to a situation of mutual support and service to the gospel and to suffering people. But the present Church vision, policy and leadership make that impossible. Nevertheless, we cannot but question and resist the priority of celibacy over mature conscience and the spirit of the gospels. We have tried to live responsibly since our contract — in separation, in jail, in legal jeopardy, in official attempts to disgrace us. Separation from our religious congregations has not been our choice for we believe in our case, as with others, celibacy is not the issue. Responsible freedom is.

They would continue to live the Gospel — "in poverty, in community, and in non-violent resistance, convinced of the contribution of religious resistance to human kind."*

It was clear from this strong, honest, unequivocal document that the Berrigans viewed their marriage as an act of civil disobedience — one intended to dramatize the outmoded and unjust character of Church requirements which made their religious dedication and service of the Gospel conditional upon their celibacy. In the journal which he kept during his trial in 1967, and subsequently published in 1970, Berrigan had once dealt with the question of married priests from a somewhat less radical standpoint. His concern then was that marriage would rob the priest of the freedom his celibacy assured him. He had seen scores of priests marry, but only one seemed to him "to have done so in freedom, to [have] become thereby a better man, a better priest." Why? "His wife shared his

* The *National Catholic Reporter*, June 8, 1973, p. 29.

grasp of the real, loving as profoundly as himself the people they served." For Berrigan, the priest must ensure the freedom demanded to preach the Gospel. To this he must subject his marriage. "Truth, charity and justice have always required that the needs of the human family have as much claim on us as the needs of our own kin — with as great a call on our service." *

Two years later, he evidently found in Elizabeth McAlister the counterpart of this strongly committed Christian woman and Berrigan married her, apparently convinced that his own freedom would in no way be abridged. When, over the course of four years, the couple could see no sign that their communities might be open to so radical an evolution in religious life, they determined to surface, whatever the cost. And obviously the cost was great for all concerned. Both orders lost strong, charismatic Christian leaders; the Church, a distinguished priest and impressive nun. Daniel Berrigan, Jesuit brother and fellow revolutionary, saw the expulsion of the two as "a sign of the retardation of religious life that [forces] some of the best people out of religious communities. In a profound sense, it is a kind of working out of the death wish of these orders." The Church might have seized on this situation to infuse new life into Christian marriage, "a totally dead scene." Instead it had laid on this union the mortmain of inflexible policy and quenched, rather than quickened, hope.†

Writing in *Win* magazine three months before the public disclosure of his marriage, Philip Berrigan made a point of the fact that Christ himself had never imposed celibacy. "And he wouldn't because he couldn't — not without doing violence to conscience." It was Christ's followers —"mystics, philosophers, bishops — who

---

* Philip Berrigan, *Prison Journals of a Priest Revolutionary* (New York: Ballantine Books, Inc., 1967), pp. 145–146.
† Daniel Berrigan in *Commonweal*, June 15, 1973, 98:326.

consistently exaggerated celibacy as a moral panacea, causing it to become, in effect, an excuse to flee from the complexities of human love." It is clear that by this point Berrigan had reasoned his way out of the necessity of celibacy as a condition of freedom. It seemed to him now simply one option among others. One could take it or leave it alone. Life-style and total Christian commitment were not coterminous. One could specify one's commitment in any number of ways. The essential thing was to live totally for the reign of Christ. And celibates had no corner on that dedication. "Our basic human problem," he concluded, "is violence against the species, a problem to be addressed equally by both the married and the celibate." *

Though the Berrigan case stunned the average Catholic and occasioned in diocesan newspapers a brief flurry of letters, pro and con the "clandestine" marriage, the fact of the matter is that a good deal of scholarly study into the origins and psychology of religious celibacy is quietly going on, together with experiments in life-style considerably to the left of the Berrigans' own position.

Sandra Schneider (an Immaculate Heart nun from Monroe, Michigan) has developed an interesting thesis which traces the distinction between celibacy and virginity to the very beginning of the Christian tradition. Speaking to a group of women religious in August of 1972, she addressed herself to the problem of identity which has perplexed nuns in the post–Vatican II period. As the Council made clear, the Gospel calls *all* Christians, not just religious, to a life of perfection: there is nothing in Revelation which validates the concept of a "higher state." And once religious congregations took *aggiornamento* seriously and dropped most of the external characteristics which set them apart, it became harder for nuns to say just who they were.

---

* Philip Berrigan in *Win* magazine, March 15, 1973, 9:41.

If their vows were not of the essence (others also live poor, separate lives totally committed to the Christian Gospel), what precisely *is* religious life? Self-evidently, said Sandra, a life that is religious. And religious people (whether or not Christian) are what they are because they are obsessed with God or the search for God. A magnificent obsession, to be sure, and irresistible as any other dominating passion, artistic, political, or broadly human. One doesn't rationally choose this compelling ideal any more than Michelangelo chose to be a painter. One is, as it were, chosen. Personality is destiny. "Because of who he is and the way he's put together [it] magnetizes all his love and all his energy in such a way that it centers his life as a keel centers a boat." Among the Jews such persons are Hasidic, among the Buddhists they are monks, among Christians they are religious who, very early in our history, appear to have practiced virginity. Virginity as a spiritual reality, not merely as the discipline of celibacy. It was not chosen "for" anything. There was no particular task set aside for Christian virgins which would have required their being celibate. "The virgin simply heard the message of Christ in such a way that marriage became an impossibility for her." Her life was so experientially filled with Jesus that "there was time and room and interest for nothing else." Significantly, she was not viewed as "unmarried" but as already married. The ceremony of her consecration as a virgin took the form of a marriage to Christ.

On the other hand, there were Christians who practiced celibacy (nonmarriage) for both ascetical and apostolic reasons — to free themselves for contemplation or for ministry in the interests of the Kingdom. But celibacy was clearly functional, a self-imposed discipline adopted to facilitate the service of one's neighbor. From these two distinct religious traditions of nonmarriage, Sandra traces descending lines to modern religious vocations, "primarily virginal" and "primarily diaconal" (service-oriented).

This is, I think, a helpful distinction, for it gives us a vocabulary to describe the very real tensions which resulted when these initially distinct callings came together in the tradition and law of the Church. Not only have successive novice mistresses interpreted the vow of chastity to mean both things — virginal union and freedom for service — but canon law itself has tended to treat the two as interchangeable. And certainly, as mentioned above, the liturgical ceremony of Reception of Habit and Profession of Vows considered all nuns Brides of Christ. Yet the word "chastity" connotes predominantly negative implications of nonsexuality and nonmarriage. And novices in my day learned more about avoiding sex than about virginity as a positive expression of love for Christ.

Though she agrees with Sandra Schneider that the historical rationale for institutionalized celibacy has been totally lost even by those practicing it, Rosemary Ruether, Howard University professor, sees the ethic of celibacy as essentially meaningless to contemporary society, since divorced from the eschatological world view which fostered it. Originally held up to all Christians as an ideal which would hasten the end of the world and the Coming of the Kingdom, celibacy now seems to her "an odd left-over from a world view which has disappeared." Its original thrust, she writes, was not really antimarriage, but sexist and narcissistic; antisex and antiprocreation. Thus, even the clergy (married since the first century of the Church) were urged by St. Jerome to live continently so as to decrease, not increase, the population and thus hurry along the end of the world. When celibacy was institutionalized among monastic orders as an ascetic way of perfection, a new rationale had to be found for it — namely, that some men were thus "gifted" by the Holy Spirit while others were not — a theology Miss Ruether rejects out of hand as inconsistent with a Scriptural view of the God of Creation.*

But if she dismisses as "antilife" an ethic which encouraged the married to live as if celibate, Miss Ruether is equally averse to the antithesis of this position today. In her estimation there is simply no way to take the old skins of institutionalized celibacy found in today's priesthood and religious orders and "pour a new wine of sexual liberation into them, keeping on the form of celibate communal life, but no longer demanding that it be a sexless life." She sees this as the direction some radical religious are pointing to. And she can only predict for it "total institutional disaster." Those she has known who have attempted such interpersonal relationships while continuing within the framework of celibate communities have "suffered destructive psychic upheavals far deeper than they expected." †

How many nuns and priests think this way I have no means of knowing. I would suspect that the number is exceedingly small. But I have met some and their position vis-à-vis celibacy seems to have been carefully and responsibly thought through. They are committed to the life they are in: they want to live a simple, communal, Christian life in service to the Kingdom. But they also want the wholeness of deep involvement with another. They see no contradiction between their vow of celibacy and such love relationships, even if these express themselves sexually. They are *not* marrying, establishing families with all the attendant responsibilities. Should they decide that they do want children, then under the present jurisdictional restrictions they *would* marry, and at that point have to leave their orders. In other words, they are taking

* Rosemary Ruether, "The Ethic of Celibacy," *Commonweal,* February 2, 1973, 97:390–394, *infra.*
† *Ibid.,* p. 393.

literally the traditional Catholic view of both celibacy (non-marriage) and marriage (union in the interests of procreation). What is truly new in such thinking is a revised notion of sin. Sexual intercourse is seen not as concubinage for the "relief of concupiscence" but as the total expression of an authentic love.

One young Jesuit graduate student makes no bones of the fact that he has such a relationship with a nun in New York City. They love each other, want to express that love, need the psychological support they give each other, consider their vow one of celibacy — a promise not to marry so as to devote themselves full-time to the service of the larger human family after the pattern of Christ. He is supported in this thinking by lots of people (students and faculty) more theologically sophisticated than most. The openness of this couple and the group acceptance they enjoy may account for the fact that neither seems to be suffering the guilt reactions Miss Ruether predicts must follow upon such radical departure from one's cultural formation. In this instance, at least, enlightened conscience seems to have escaped guilt feelings. If one can trust the evidence one sees in the lives of many reflective Catholics, they are not alone in their serenity.

Other less radical young nuns and priests do not go this far but feel it essential to growth to have both male and female friends. They want the right to spend time together, to relax together, to take in a movie and go out to dinner. Wearing modern dress, living alone or in groups with similar outlooks, they enjoy the anonymity which readily facilitates this "normal" kind of life-style. To Catholics in general and to older religious used to notions of cloister, this mode of life looks uncomfortably like dating — in America a convention viewed as preparatory to marriage. It's hard for such persons to accept the new patterns. They feel that religious life is somewhat compromised and wish that young people would just "be one thing or another." They cannot deal with the degree of ambiguity which is the natural climate of the young.

The story is told that when Elizabeth Taylor's director wanted to prepare her for the death scene in *Cleopatra,* he walked into her dressing room casually stroking a harmless but enormous snake. As he hoped, Miss Taylor fainted dead away. When she came to and saw only a tiny garter snake instead, she grasped it to her bosom with relief if not with pleasure.

Infelicitous as the image may be, it suggests to me an analogy for the feelings of indignant Catholics reading of the secret marriage contracted by Philip Berrigan and Elizabeth McAlister. A "spoiled nun" and a "spoiled priest" compounding their defections by marrying while still under vows. Juxtaposed with the Jesuit from New York, the Berrigans may seem conservative indeed!

CHAPTER TEN

NEW WINE INTO
OLD SKINS

History shows that as fast as institutionalized
religion decays, it has the power of reviving.
— GORDON ALLPORT

Psychologists today speak of a new generation coming into existence every seven years. As Toffler has pointed out to us, the modern
world is rushing into the future with such dizzying speed that we
are reeling from future shock. I felt its impact every time I caught a
plane back to Chicago from Mississippi. In the tiny little Catholic
community that centered on the campus Newman chapel, there was
liturgical evidence that Vatican II had happened. (Father faced the
congregation during Mass, experimented with an occasional
dialogue-sermon, even introduced dance at the Offertory.) But by
and large nobody was much rocking the boat where Mother Church
was concerned. There were, to be sure, nuns in Natchez, Vicksburg,
Jackson. But, buried in the depths of rural Mississippi, I never got
to know them.

Back in Chicago for Thanksgiving or Christmas, or educational or
literary meetings, I sensed the speed with which changes were con-

tinuing, far faster than even I had anticipated when I had grasped my freedom and journeyed south. The process of evolution with its inevitable confusions, struggles, and tensions was almost visibly apparent. It wasn't merely that the press was filled with stories of priests and nuns asking for laicization and marrying (frequently each other), it was that so many of the nuns were members of my own congregation. (The current joke among diocesan clergy was said to be that BVM's made better teachers, but Mercy's better wives!)

In innumerable ways, the nuns I knew were, like myself, consciously reaching out for new patterns, fresh ways of defining themselves and their relationships to others, new images by which to communicate to themselves their refurbished sense of who they were, where they were going. Among some Chicago BVM's I heard talk of forming a new region to bring together people who wanted to keep alive the momentum of the post–Vatican II years. They feared not the rapidity but the possible paralysis of change. The old symbols which had once bound us together in characteristically uniform communities seemed to be coming apart. People were clustering for new reasons, some of which they could not themselves quite articulate. There was nothing neat about the whole thing, no clear metaphysical framework that I could discern. It was somehow like being in at the birth of new, inchoate myths, the old ones having proved brittle or inadequate and having been shattered, exploded, or at least lost along the way. I began to pay close attention to surface indicators — listening to the talk, peering between the lines of news accounts and chance personal encounters, trying to discern the trends, to assess the meaning.

What I saw was fascinating: nuns in large numbers were drifting away from the schools, moving into the public sector of society, cutting across congregational lines to merge forces around issues which deeply concerned them. Some nuns were joining the system to change it from within; others (frequently their own colleagues) were rejecting the system to dramatize its hollowness. Nuns were moving into living groups where they could experience shared prayer; others were moving out of the same houses because they wanted no part of spontaneous prayer meetings. The Pentecostal movement was beginning to surface and to claim growing numbers. Prayer and its place in the life of religious was becoming a centrifugal question for groups which had once formed along lines of corporate work. On this constantly shifting scene even the language was new.

Vatican II had fairly deluged the Catholic world with ecclesiastical jargon. Eventually even the popular press began to bristle with "Vaticanese" as week by week *Time* magazine carried the latest reports to a curiously interested public. But the words I was hearing now were different — words like ministry, charisma, incarnationalism, theology of liberation or of hope, resistance, power. I found myself beginning to sort out nuns not as Franciscans, BVM's, Dominicans but as politically oriented, resistance-minded, charismatic, traditionalist. The key word, perhaps, was *ministry,* a word nuns had not previously used in self-definition.

When I entered the congregation, we spoke in terms of our *apostolate* (ours was education). Other nuns made nursing or missionary work their chief focus. (We called our local houses "missions" but this was only because we were "sent" there by superiors.) For most of us today these terms sound old-fashioned, freighted with overtones of proselytism, of carrying the Good News to the faithless, to the heathen sitting in outer darkness (an image which always conveyed to me as a child the notion of a gang of natives lolling around the island till the Christians found them!). Today Sisters tend to think in terms of ministry, the work of listen-

ing to and responding to the needs of persons, whatever these may be. Ministry is life-giving, concerned with the freeing of others. The new modes of pastoral ministry — the work with prisoners, drug addicts, the elderly, minority groups, the poor — are directed not toward saving souls but toward helping people to become more *human,* helping to make the world a better place to live in. But humanness, in the Christian context, implies a constant relation and interaction among God, man, and the world. So ministry, I discovered, was spilling over even into what was hitherto the no-man's-land of politics. The first BVM I heard about out there was Sister Nellie Forsyth, an Iowa delegate to the 1972 National Democratic Convention. Not everyone in the congregation saw this as ministry, I'm certain. She must at least have raised a few Republican eyebrows! But in no time so many other congregations were crowding the scene that Nellie seemed quite tame. Sister Ann Gillen ran a successful campaign for the national governing board of Common Cause. Sister Loretta Ann Madden of Colorado registered as a lobbyist at the state capital with the announced goal "to watch legislation which affects the quality of human life." * Sister Clare Dunn is running for election to the state House of Representatives in Arizona and Sister Mary Ann Guthrie is a candidate for the Democratic nomination to Tennessee's Eighth Congressional District seat in the House, the first nun to try for the United States Congress.†
At a time when, from an ethical point of view, American public life seems conspicuously threadbare, it is hard to see how the presence of politically competent nuns can do anything but improve the quality of the Congress.

Admittedly, nuns in politics are as yet only a tiny minority. There

* The *National Catholic Reporter,* February 22, 1974, p. 2.
† Sister Dunn ran a successful campaign and is currently serving in the Arizona state legislature. Sister Mary Ann Guthrie lost her bid for the nomination.

are still thousands of nuns running hospitals and teaching in parochial schools — though not so many as a decade ago, certainly, when nuns so dominated the Catholic school system that parents commonly referred to "sending the kids to the Sisters." Although we tend to forget the fact, there was always a sprinkling of lay teachers who were perceived as an exciting anomaly. ("Mama — there's a real *lady* teaching the third grade this year!") Today the situation is almost directly reversed. To the dismay of pre–Vatican II Catholics, who feel somehow cheated if Johnny doesn't "have a Sister," lay teachers now outnumber the nuns. In many Chicago parochial schools, it is Sister who is excitingly different. ("She's not Miss *anybody;* she's Sister Sally Davis.")

If there are proportionately fewer nuns, however, there appear to be significantly more of them in decision-making positions. When nuns were plentiful, they not only staffed the school but often served as convent housekeepers and cooks. (The only two I can think of now work for Meals on Wheels!) Today the single nun left in a parish plant may be the grade-school principal. Where there are others, interestingly enough, they may turn out to be from different congregations. The day when certain schools were, in effect, "franchised" to one religious congregation, which supplied all needed staff, are just about over. Like their lay counterparts, nuns now tend to apply to diocesan or parish hiring boards for grade- and high-school faculty positions in Catholic schools. If they no longer wear habits which differentiate them, if they tend to live in communal groups near the school where they teach, I suspect that it will not be long before nuns in intercongregational situations will call into question the artificial barriers which separate them. The possibility of community mergers seems not only likely but inevitable.

But though nuns have by no means abandoned Catholic schools

and colleges, I do see them moving into other institutions. There are nuns teaching and counseling in public school systems. There are nuns with faculty rank at Yale, Barnard, Indiana, Union Theological, St. Louis, and other leading universities. At times they are on leave from community-owned Catholic colleges. Often they are on permanent appointment. There are dozens of nuns teaching in southern black colleges and universities — Atlanta, Emory, Jackson State, Livingston. Some went originally to integrate the faculties and help such schools comply with HEW guidelines. Many have stayed on with tenure, convinced that this is where they can best exercise their personal ministry.

What interests me even more is the fact that in Church institutions and organizations nuns have begun to fill administrative and executive positions once the preserve of the clergy. Sister Elinor Ford is superintendent of schools in the New York archdiocese. Sister Agnes Cunningham is a director of the Catholic Theological Society of America. Sister Dorothy Donnelly, who heads the two-thousand-member National Coalition of American Nuns, is a faculty member in the Jesuit School of Theology at Berkeley. Sister Teresa Avila MacLeod, director of Rome's Regina Mundi school of theology for women, is a member of the Vatican Congregation for Religious Secular Institutes. Granted that these are rare birds indeed, this kind of visibility for nuns seems to me an encouraging sign of thawing at the tip of the ecclesiastical glacier.

At the sacramental level of ministry, nevertheless, I do not perceive nuns to have yet made the tiniest dent. Agnes Cunningham and Teresa MacLeod, as well as any number of male Catholic theologians, have made it abundantly clear that there are really no Biblical or doctrinal objections to ordaining women. The circular reasoning by which a male-dominated Church maintains its obviously sexist position vis-à-vis the priesthood has long since been exposed. The St. Joan's International Alliance is waging a vigorous campaign for female ordination; canon lawyer Claire Henning has again and again told national audiences that she wants not only to be ordained but to be elected Pope. But nuns have remained singularly silent with regard to this last exclusively male stronghold within the Church. There are nuns superbly qualified to function as priests, to serve as spiritual directors for congregations of women. They could quickly move toward that goal if the Church made it available. But they will not fight for it. It is a curious and intriguing phenomenon. Is it that the ancient tradition of Mary as handmaid has been so thoroughly internalized by the present generation of nuns that they cannot imagine themselves in this sacred capacity? I suspect that this may be true of many older nuns. But it is less likely to characterize the under-thirty group. Sister Carol Ann Kemp of St. Gabriel's in Washington, D.C., responded quite differently when I asked her if she'd like to be ordained: "Not with the present status of the clergy!" * Having so recently weathered the struggle for freedom from rigid rules and superiors, nuns like Carol Ann tend to view with alarm the even more formidable citadel of the rectory, the pastor, the bishop. They rightly see the diocesan clergy as far less free than they themselves are.

Among the very young, there appears to be a growing number of women looking toward ordination in the future. Under pressure, some Catholic seminaries have already admitted women who want to be ready when the time is ripe. Now that the Episcopal Church in Philadelphia has ordained eleven women priests, Catholic women seminarians may finally insist that the Church literally achieve its vaunted wholeness in which there is "neither Jew nor Greek, neither slave nor free, neither male nor female." Even Pope

* Interview with the author, Washington, D.C., January 5, 1974.

Paul VI has called for "a progressive equalization of the basic rights of men and women," terming the progress of women "foreseeable, possible, and desirable." * The ordination of women, I am convinced, will come. To my mind, the only question is *when.*

Theologian Dorothy Donnelly has suggested that the Holy Spirit has the answer to that question, since she thinks it is He who is moving the Church along in what she considers a "natural" step. That same Holy Spirit, she says, is propelling nuns out of the schools they have traditionally run and into new ministries. "This great bird — the Holy Spirit — is out here calling women, giving them the gifts of ministry." And the Church ought to be confirming, not suppressing, these gifts. "The Spirit is not famous for following the lead of the magisterium," she warns. "Women have got to realize that power is good and can well be used to help society." Anticipating the emergence of women into pastoral ministry, Professor Donnelly sets her seminary graduate students of both sexes to grapple with the problems of revitalizing the moral life of American business and reforming the American prison system. The goal of Christian ministry, ordained or not, must be the building of a better world.†

This view, that the business of the Christian is to build the Kingdom here and now, has a peculiarly post–Vatican II ring for most Catholics, some of whom are just now beginning to think in terms of a theology of hope and who may still not be totally comfortable with the notion of priests in Congress, a Jesuit in the White House. In the traditional Church (the one I grew up in) a Christian fled the world. Wherever the hierarchy stood, religious priests and nuns led ascetical lives which had nothing in common with Watergate apartments and seats of power. Gradually, however, the eschatology

* *New York Times,* November 18, 1973, p. 13.
† Dorothy Donnelly in the *National Catholic Reporter,* November 23, 1973.

of Moltmann, the incarnationalism of Cooke, the phenomenology of de Chardin are seeping through to the practical level where actions are taken. An increasing number of nuns do hold to a belief that human beings share in the creating of a better society, that the world is truly evolutionary, that out of the struggle for survival a stronger, more perfect society will emerge, that the Kingdom (if anywhere) is here and now. They work that this Kingdom may come.

Not all nuns share this vision of involvement, however. For a not insignificant number, it is the power of prayer rather than political power which will create the Kingdom. This has of course always been true of the contemplative orders which, despite some updating of their life-style, continue to place primary emphasis on the ministry of prayer. But now (along with running schools and hospitals) some active orders are opening houses of retreat and prayer as well. And this not merely to meet the demands of their own members but also those of a steadily growing number of lay people with a deep interest in reflection and shared prayer and a desire to participate at some level in a profoundly spiritual life.

Even more surprising to me has been the startling growth of Pentecostalism among Catholics during the past half-dozen years. I remember first hearing about this when it surfaced at Duquesne University late in the sixties. For a while the novelty of it all dominated the attention of Catholic journalists. We read that spontaneous prayer was catching on among students. There were articles about public healing (the laying on of hands), about "glossolalia," or speaking in tongues. For my taste it all had a too decidedly Protestant, revivalist flavor. Certainly it was nothing I could relate to. Then the phenomenon spread to Notre Dame University and a number of priests and some nuns were drawn into the movement. Today the Charismatic Movement (as its adherents prefer to call it) looks like a major force in American life. It has the support of no less a personage than Cardinal Suenens and claims the allegiance of hundreds of priests, lay Catholics, and nuns — among them an indeterminate number of BVM's.

Mundelein's Sister Marina Kennelly, for one, is a "leader" in a charismatic community, "People of the Resurrection," which includes a group of families with their children as well as some university students — about forty persons in all. The group meets alternately on the campus of Chicago's Loyola University and in St. Jerome's parish center. I sought out Marina for the express purpose of getting myself invited to a charismatic service. We ended up in a frank and thoroughly enlightening discussion of the meaning of the movement.

Actually I had a whole range of questions I wanted to raise with Marina, for hers has been a unique spiritual odyssey. Five years ago, after some twenty as a BVM, she left Mundelein (where she had chaired the department of chemistry) to enter the contemplative life of the Carmelites. The attempt, I knew, had been disappointing, for after only two months she returned to the college and took up where she had left off. Now I asked her candidly why she had gone to Carmel in the first place. And, having worked so hard for change in our own congregation, I could not miss the irony of her response.

"Well, I felt that the BVM's — like most nuns in the sixties — were concentrating on *external* renewal. I had serious doubts that we could in the long run survive."

"And at Carmel — what did you find?"

(She reacts with an expressive shrug.)

"An intensely literal living of the Rule. An eighty-three-year-old nun steps out of line and is publicly corrected. The prioress fears that if small deviations are permitted, the whole discipline is threatened." (Her intense blue eyes cloud over.) "It was de-humanizing to me. So I left."

Back in Chicago, she had quite literally stumbled upon the charismatic movement.

"Someone invited me to go to a prayer meeting. I went. And it changed my whole life."

"But what have you found that you did not find at Carmel — the 'felt' experience of God?"

"Yes. And peace. And joy."

(I think as I look at her that she needn't have told me; it is so evident.)

"The Scriptures have come alive for me. And the Eucharist is far more meaningful. I feel, too, that I see people as the Lord sees them — as expressions of Him. Even penance has grown in meaning. It gets at the root of the problem, you see. Psychiatry may *identify* the problem. But penance *heals* the memory."

(I plunge in.)

"But why the speaking in tongues? What is that all about?"

"It's just that we want to praise the Lord in as many ways as possible. And we run out of words! So the Spirit supplies them for us. The language may be modern, ancient, even preconceptual. But it is not known to the person speaking it. It has to be translated, even to the one praying."

"You take this to be a kind of prophecy, then?"

"At times, yes. For the Spirit comes only through the group. *Community* is the note on which the Spirit is coming into the Church today. To really live the Christian life, we have, under His guidance, to reject the values of the world. Through the love of the community a new order will emerge."

"So you feel that your prayers are answered?"

(Her smile is swift, compassionate.)

"Of course. And I never really felt this before. For so long we prayed in the words of other people, not our own."

"You mean that we 'said' prayers or recited the Office."

"Yes. And we never expected to see the results until the next life." (She brightens.) "But now I do expect results. We believe that when your life is right your prayers *are* answered. But the fundamental relationships have to be right first — brother with brother, sister with sister."

"Catch-22!" (It's irreverent, but I can't resist.) She describes to me a German charismatic community of nuns who run a large printing establishment outside Berlin. It was founded about twenty-five years ago in atonement for World War II. Whenever there is a lack of charity among these nuns, the printing press gets fouled up and stops. Mechanics can find nothing wrong. So the community gathers and looks into their hearts. They pray. And the machines start up! She opens her hands and smiles.

I learn, too, that there are charismatic houses among contemplatives and that, contrary to criticism, charismatic communities do have a social aspect. But members are encouraged to participate in existing social-action groups, not to form their own. Their strategy is to change the social structure gradually through the witness of community, of person, not through the use of power.

"What about the criticism I've heard — that the movement draws a lot of kooks?" (She's heard this too and smiles disparagingly.)

"Where else will they go? We do attract people with problems. But we recognize that help comes from the Lord. For these people with problems as well as for others. Maybe this is what attracts them."

She describes with enthusiasm the nonresident household of which she is a member: Sam Hilburn and his wife and their three children, and two other young couples. Everyone meets for dinner and for prayer two or three times a week or oftener. The bond among them is obviously deep and caring. I ask if the logical next step is not a resident community. My question uncovers the fact that there are already nuns living in charismatic households. Some because they have experienced a crisis in their own religious life: there is no community — and no desire for it on the part of many; no liturgy — and no desire for it; no common or shared prayer — and no desire for it.

"Do you think there is hope for religious life?"

"Only if there is a complete renewal in the Spirit." *

It is a charismatic note on which to end the interview and we do. But my speculations are just beginning. Tough old rationalist that I am, I can only stand outside the magic circle of Pentecostalism. I did not come to scoff. But neither can I stay to pray. I must take seriously this experience I cannot share, however, for though its possible influence on religious life is still to be determined, it seems to cast a long shadow before it.

Still, the contemplatives, the charismatics, represent only a fraction of American nuns. Most pursue a more traditional style of personal prayer while they throw their energies into the rebuilding of the secular city. The majority still teach, or nurse, or do social work. But more and more are showing up in quite unexpected jobs. I know of a nun who is an executive secretary to a psychiatrist, one who runs a storefront community center, another who is a scientific researcher for an electronics firm. Sister Rita Benz left teaching for public relations, got herself an internship with a New York advertising agency, then accepted a full-time job with Public Communications Inc. in Chicago. Though it may not always like it, the public

* Interview with the author, Chicago, January 13, 1974.

is getting used to the idea of a nun medical officer in the navy or even toting a gun for the FBI. A significant number of nuns are going into law as a mode of public service (frequently in the interests of minorities and the poor). Sister Patricia Donovan is deputy attorney general for the Commonwealth of Pennsylvania; Sister Catherine Ryan is assistant state's attorney for Cook County, Chicago.

Not everyone is unreservedly happy about this burgeoning of careers among nuns. Even they themselves have occasional reservations about the "apostolic" character of some of these new works and from time to time review their activities in the light of the Church's mission of justice and peace. But what has really unnerved some segments of the public (and certain bishops) is nuns on the other side of the law — those I admiringly term "resistance-minded." They *are* something new under the American sun. They promote fuel boycotts; they walk picket lines with the United Farm Workers; they throw themselves into the aisles of St. Patrick's Cathedral during Sunday Mass to protest American military policies and the failure of their Church to criticize these.

In pre–Vatican II country, this was unheard of. Nuns had seemed the very symbol of orthodoxy and tradition, models of reverence and compliance. The Vietnam War changed all this. Sister Caren Lydon, one of five New York Sisters of Charity who invaded St. Patrick's on May 1, 1972, admitted to Edward Fiske of the *Times* that she had acted on her own, without permission of her superiors. "We felt a sense of urgency about the escalation of the bombing and what it was doing to people. The Church always talks about the right to life. We felt that as a body of women we should address the Church on the same point." *

* *New York Times,* May 8, 1972.

Nuns who have taken similar positions and faced the cold disapproval of pastors, the ostracism of fellow religious, the criticism of conservative Catholics, will easily imagine the kinds of reactions Sister Caren and her friends encountered. But week after week, month after month, stories of this sort continue to show up in the media. And bit by bit a new image of the nun takes shape — the nun as conscienticized, individually responsible, willing to take risks in the name of Christian commitment. The nun as one with the existential courage to choose.

In Latin America nuns working for social justice have been consistently harried and, in some cases, very roughly handled. A rioting mob of self-styled "anti-Communists" demolished the house of the Religious Sisters of the Assumption in Argentina a year ago. The real object of this attack was apparently the Third World Movement, a liberal organization in which the nuns have been active.*
Mary Harding, an American Maryknoll nun sent to Bolivia in 1959, is reported to have been jailed and tortured for refusing to reveal information regarding her associates in the Army of National Liberation, a guerrilla offshoot of Che Guevara's revolutionary movement. According to a story in the *New York Times*, Miss Harding left her order four years ago so as not to compromise it by her political activity. In January of 1973, she was described by the State Department as the only American political prisoner being held in Bolivia.† Her experience suggests how tenuous is the position of religious congregations which get involved in the fight for humanization.

In this country, resistance to the war in Vietnam and concern to create a world free of oppression have brought other nuns into American courtrooms and jails. Probably no one was better publicized in

---

* The *Catholic Messenger*, August 23, 1973, p. 2.
† *New York Times*, January 11, 1973.

this respect than Elizabeth McAlister. Indicted as one of the Harrisburg Seven on charges of conspiracy to kidnap Henry Kissinger and blow up heating units in Washington public buildings, she narrowly escaped jail. Others did not. Sister Jogues Egan (once Elizabeth McAlister's provincial) was sentenced to York County Jail for contempt of court during the Harrisburg trial; Sister Carol Jegen and a score of nun-companions spent two weeks behind bars in August of 1973 for picketing with Cesar Chavez's Chicano workers in Delano, California. Dozens of other nuns have risked harassment, arrest, trial, and conviction in the interest of justice for others.

Resistance to power rather than the co-opting of it is the obvious strategy here. And this wherever power is unjustly wielded — by Government or by Church, for both are seen as frequently oppressive within their own domains. And there is no hesitation about so labeling them. There are, to be sure, comparatively few nuns among the ranks of the civilly disobedient. But then prophets are always in notoriously short supply.

Quite as interesting as the daring avant-garde who make the brilliant, often unprogrammed breaks through the lines is the whole panoply of politically oriented groups I see functioning as backup troops. Their obvious goal is to channel the enormous power until recently latent in American nuns. Some of these are official: the Leadership Conference of Women Religious (LCWR) grew out of the old Conference of Major Superiors set up by the Sacred Congregation in 1957. Most are grass-roots organizations formed since the Council to tackle one or another issue of national significance. In addition to the National Association of Women Religious, there are, for instance, the National Coalition of American Nuns (NCAN), Las Hermanas, the Black Sisters Coalition, and Network. The major theme with most of these groups is justice for the

184

oppressed and they operate in overlapping areas with a nice shade of creative conflict. All the grass-roots organizations happily have representation in the Leadership Conference where, like friendly watchdogs, they nip and tug at superiors lest they neglect the opinion of the hoi polloi.

Quite frankly a lobbying operation, Network operates out of Washington, D.C. Since February of 1972 it has been lifting the sights of nuns regarding legislation for human rights at every level — local, national, international. Its well-written quarterly focuses on problems of social justice such as prison reform, world food shortages, the Equal Rights Amendment. Since Network's aim is to get Sisters actively involved in task forces dealing with specific problems, it is program-oriented and organized by congressional district, not by diocese. Network has caught the attention of Senators Stevenson, Hatfield, and Humphrey as well as of congressional representatives, Common Cause, and the League of Women Voters. Sister Marjorie Tuite, Illinois representative to Network, explicates its political theology as "the Beatitudes times twentieth-century technology."

NCAN is small (some eighteen hundred members) and "snarky." Its executive director, Sister Ann Gillen, called insistently for the impeachment of Nixon, seeing the erosion of public confidence in his administration as a critical national problem. NCAN takes strong positions on Church matters as well and doesn't mince words. When Archbishop James J. Byrne of Dubuque, Iowa, was named liaison with the leadership conference, NCAN's newsletter criticized Byrne as a bad choice. It accused him of quashing the grass-roots organization of the nuns in his own diocese and charged him with bias in favor of the Consortium Perfectae Caritatis (an association of nuns who retain strictly traditional forms of religious life).* In language which bore no trace of nunnish obsequiousness, the coalition chided the National Conference of Catholic Bishops for their "boo, boo, which this time certainly cannot be Rosemary's." †

In all the galaxy of acronyms by which Sisters refer to their national organizations, none seems more influential than the Leadership Conference. Its current head is Sister Francis Borgia Rothluebber, a deceptively soft-spoken woman of formidable credentials. Having steered her own Franciscan congregation through the shoals of renewal in the late sixties, she has no illusions about the attitudes of the Sacred Congregation toward the autonomy of American nuns. "They simply *do not accept* equality, shared responsibility, authority as vested in the members of the community who in turn delegate a share of this authority to their superiors." ‡

Summoned to Rome to justify her order's elimination of local superiors in favor of a democratic decision-making process, she found herself in a monumental struggle with the Sacred Congregation. Typically, she did not receive a clear decision. Instead, they designated this move "experimental"— a term which indicates that the matter will be reexamined in Rome at the close of the twelve-year suspension of canon law enacted by the Vatican Council.

Listening to her shrewd analysis of Church politics during a lengthy interview this spring, I felt confident that Francis Borgia will successfully deflect any attempt of the Sacred Congregation to reintroduce pyramidal structures of authority into American congregations of women. She sees this as a crucial issue. "If we can, as

---

* The name is derived from a Vatican Council document on religious life, *Perfectae Caritatis* (*Decree on the Adaptation and Renewal of Religious Life, October, 1965*).
† See, for example, the *National Catholic Reporter,* January 18, 1974, p. 3.
‡ Interview with the author, Milwaukee, Wisconsin, January 28, 1974.

women, hold on to our decision-making groups and modify hierarchical patterns, we will cause the biggest revolution in the concept of authority the Church has ever seen." *

Though by no means monolithic in its attitudes, the Leadership Conference today clearly reflects its president's liberal outlook on Church affairs and Christian responsibilities. When I found on my arrival in Washington that Dom Helder Camara was the centerpiece of the August, 1973, meeting of the group, I knew that he was no random choice. His low-keyed, strongly charismatic plea to American nuns to focus their energies on a "Year of Justice" was followed up by Francis Borgia's outline of what she sees as the threefold goal of the conference: justice, liberation, and the humanization of persons. And she made it clear that these have global and not merely national implications.

Admittedly there is also a strong conservative element in the LCWR, some of it almost certainly traceable to the habited members of the Consortium within its ranks. Now an international organization with members in fourteen nations, this movement started out as an effort among some American nuns to achieve renewal without radically changing the traditional principles or external customs of religious life. Needless to say, the group does not endorse any deep social involvement by nuns nor does it push for the ordination of women. I would expect it to be chilly toward the passage of the Equal Rights Amendment as well.† Francis Borgia, however, sees a growing awareness among nuns generally as they belatedly tie in with the women's movement. It is a trend she applauds.

In view of their own oppression by the Church, and considering their numbers, the properties they control, and their geographical

---

* *Ibid.*
† *The National Catholic Reporter,* March 22, 1974.

scatter, nuns stand to make a considerable contribution to the movement. Some, like Sisters Austin Dougherty (a founder of NOW) and Albertus Magnus McGrath (author of a recent history of women in the Church),* have long been active proponents of liberation. And Sister Joel Read, dynamic young president of Alverno College, has established on that campus a center for research in women's studies. It is my impression that most nuns need to widen their perspectives in this regard. As a group long out of the mainstream of competitive life, they often do not see the full dimensions of the oppression of women in our society. One reason for this may be that, along with its undeniable historical condescension to women, the Church can also claim a long record of female exaltation in the person of Mary. This fact, together with its emphasis on the dignity of Christian motherhood, has rather successfully obscured its generally androcentric character. Then, too, having bypassed marriage, and having traditionally stood outside the scramble for pay and jobs, nuns are slow to think of themselves as sexually exploited.

This picture is rapidly changing, however. Since Vatican II, the absolute numbers of Sisters in the United States has declined sharply — in some orders by as much as 30 percent. As a result, nuns are pressing hard on pastors and bishops to bring their stipends to a realistic level, one which will enable them to support their retired members as well as to maintain their own professional competence. Nothing, I have observed, is apt to raise the level of consciousness among nuns quite so fast as the discovery of a double pay standard for Sisters and priests teaching in the same school.

The report of the Eastern Task Force on Women Religious in the Church published in October, 1973, revealed that there is indeed great bias against nuns. When diocesan jobs are filled, priests in-

* Sister Albertus Magnus McGrath, O.P., *What a Modern Catholic Believes about Women* (Chicago: Thomas More Press, 1972).

variably get the edge — and this despite the fact that nuns are frequently better qualified and have records of proven effectiveness. The report disclosed widespread indignation among nuns over the naming of college sophomore Deborah Shellman to the Vatican Commission on Women. It labeled the method of selecting commission members "non-participative, secretive, and discriminatory." *

Feminist writers like Mary Daly and Betty Friedan are also penetrating the thinking of nuns. When I met with Ms. Friedan following her interview with Pope Paul VI, she was surprisingly optimistic about the position of women vis-à-vis the Church. She thinks we will prove to be a historic watershed in the long chronicle of Christianity. She admitted, though, that she was shocked to see the views of women represented at the Vatican only through men. In her opinion only when women get into the offices where their own fate is determined will substantial changes be made. Women have got to step into decision-making spots on the Commission on Birth Control, the Commission on Women in the Church, the marriage courts.

Sister Francis Borgia couldn't agree more. She is personally indignant at the sexist character of the Church's language both in the Liturgy and in official documents. " 'Pray, brethren' is intolerable!" she exclaims. "One has only to think of a woman speaking to five hundred men and stretching out her hands to them, saying, 'Pray, Sisters.' You'd hear the guffaw from here to New York." †

As titular head of some 140,000 American nuns, Francis Borgia has a unique perspective. How would she describe the position of nuns with regard to the values of our secularized society generally?

---

* *Women Religious in the Church*, ed. Dolores C. Pomerlau (Washington, D.C.: Center for Concern, October, 1973), p. 15.
† Interview with the author, January 28, 1974.

"Ambivalent." Her hands underscore the dilemma. "How can one be for and against at the same time? If you say, 'I reject out of hand the twentieth-century industrial-economic-educational world,' you're rejecting out of hand some very fine developments. So the call is to *affirm,* not to reject. Of course it's simpler to say, 'I'm going to leave it all and live with the destitute as a destitute person.' But that attitude has to be deromanticized, demythologized. One has to use the technology of the age one lives in to affirm the perennial Christian values. And yet one has somehow to confront power with powerlessness, confident it will overcome." *

This way of putting it gives shape to the elusive image of the new nun I have been reaching out for. In the tumultuous years since the Council, she has indeed been demythologized, deromanticized. (I think of all those dust-gathering Chambers prints, all those pastel photographs of the Little Flower gazing serenely down from convent parlor walls: *Withered stumps of time.* Displaced symbols of a nineteenth-century nunnish ideal.)

The post–Vatican II nun, I realize, cannot be captured in a static metaphor. She is be-coming. Once a comfortable otherworldly sign of unalterable faith, she functions today as a prickly, frequently unwelcome reminder of what society would like to forget — the disjointed post-Christian character of our times and the responsibilities we all share for this.

The Council was indeed a kind of Pandora's box. Out of it flew more disorder, upheaval, and radical change than any of us in the Church had bargained for. Now that the dust of the past decade is settling, we can assess the scene. There are fewer nuns; on the surface they look and live like everyone else. More sophisticated, better educated, thoroughly committed, in some cases highly politicized

* *Ibid.*

—they no longer come across as people passively taking orders, but as persons in charge of their own lives. They are not people without burning questions; they are people passionately in search of ultimate meaning and the transforming values it holds for society.

Pouring new wine into old skins is a dangerous business. But this is what the new nuns are up to.

CHAPTER ELEVEN

GOING AND COMING

AIRLINE PILOT: *"We're lost, but we're making damn good time!"*

Will the institution of religious life survive into the twenty-first century? Daniel Berrigan says no, not unless it opens itself to the reality of a radically new mode of existence. To reject its finest and best merely because they choose to marry is, in his opinion, to express an unconscious death wish. Theologian Gabriel Moran agrees. He's been telling religious congregations how dead they are for the past four years. "We've got to face it while we still have enough concerned people left in the movement to crystallize new, living forms of community." * For Rosemary Reuther, one thing at least is certain: new forms of community will not grow out of the celibate rectory or the convent. "There must be a radical and thorough-going thinking through of a new world view in all its dimensions, and the development of a new social form of human

---

* *Jackson Daily News,* May 12, 1973, p. 9.

relationships that will really be adequate and suitable to contain such a world view." * To Malachi Martin (quondam Jesuit Vatican official) the situation is more dire than any of these views suggest. In his opinion, the Church itself is "petrified," "mummified," "desiccated." Like a crocodile it has no future — it is a "creature which will not evolve beyond its present state." Moreover, it is Jesus Himself who has reduced the Church to this moribund condition. Thus, it is "healthier to live without a religious community than to dwell in a posthumous church." †

There is no question that the avalanche of changes over the past decade took American religious congregations by surprise. We had naïvely expected that our institutions, our social arrangements, would endure indefinitely. We were really not prepared for sudden change. When our roles were shattered, our sense of who we were was endangered. But religious congregations are now familiar with the shifting forces of history. In retrospect they ask themselves which of the many sources of change were deliberate and conscious. They realize that though it is too soon to assess the effectiveness of the changes, some of these have indeed been so radical that they do seem to spell the end of an era. But, whatever may be the fate of religious orders in the future, for thousands of their members, this special world has indeed ended. In the seven-year period between 1966 and 1973, about three thousand priests left their religious orders, nearly the same number of Brothers left, and the number of nuns declined by almost 20 percent from 181,421 to 146,914.‡

Why this unprecedented decimation of the ranks? The explanation one probably hears most frequently advanced is the desire to marry. But I suspect that the reasons why anyone leaves religious

---

* *Commonweal,* February 2, 1973, 97: 394.
† *Chicago Sun Times,* December 8, 1973, p. 58.
‡ *Jackson Daily News,* May 12, 1973, p. 9.

life are complex and nuanced. When I was projecting this book and listed peace activist Elizabeth McAlister as someone I wanted to interview, she was a nun teaching art history at New York City's Marymount College. When I met her in Baltimore last December, she was the expectant wife of Philip Berrigan and living in a mixed commune called Jonah's House — a rented old brownstone in a black neighborhood. When I began to write, Sister Elizabeth McCormack was the distinguished president of Manhattanville College. This fall she announced her decision to leave both the presidency (after eight years) and the Society of the Sacred Heart (after thirty years). She was already Ms. Elizabeth McCormack affiliated with the Rockefeller Brothers Fund when we met in New York this spring.

By 1973, three of the four nuns David Susskind had interviewed as "New Nuns" in 1966 had left their congregations: Sister Jacqueline Grennan became Mrs. Paul Wexler and president of Hunter College; Sister Charles Borromeo joined Mundelein's theology department as Dr. Mary Ellen Muckinhern; Sister Kristen Morrison married John Kunnenkeri and was named dean of Newton College.

Last August, I myself returned to private life as Mary Griffin and took up where I had left off three years earlier in Mundelein's English department. The day I signed my indult of secularization I had been a professed nun for thirty-one years.

Why do nuns leave? Elizabeth McAlister because she was too avant-garde: her congregation could not assimilate her marriage and her husband. Wearing blue-and-white houndstooth pants and plum-colored socks, she curled up on one leg, knitting away at an enormous sweater ("my way of giving up smoking") as we talked. No, she had not wanted to leave her congregation. She did not ask for a dispensation. In fact, once the news of her marriage broke, she wrote a letter saying she did not intend to request a dispensation. But it came anyway. And she signed it. In Philip's case, he asked for no dispensation, nor did he sign one. So technically he is still a member of the Josephite Fathers.

I wonder how she interpreted religious life that she saw no incongruity in her decision to marry Philip while remaining a nun.

"That the vow of chastity did not forbid love. On the contrary that it encouraged that. And therefore very deep love. What I saw as a dividing line was establishing the home-family kind of setup which would demand a certain exclusivity in relationship which at that time, and even at this time, we don't possess. I'm gone four days a week at least."

It would have been more conventional to have freed oneself from one commitment before taking on another. She chose not to do that. Why had she felt this was not necessary?

"I don't know, truly, at what point the thinking began. The concept of the mixed community has always been an interesting concept to me. Why is one form of life more religious than another? ... The relationship between celibacy and sexuality — what does it mean? Does that compromise a religious commitment? Or does it make one a better, contributing member of the community? What I saw as the difference was if you just separated yourself from that and set up a home. That's a physical separation and also a psychic separation. But we both chose to maintain that connectedness, to maintain that life-style.

"In terms of what I saw as priorities within the religious community — priorities of the Gospel and priority of sharing, public witness, and all of that, I saw that these were enhanced and by no means negated by this other commitment. I was a full member of the community and a contributing member of that community. We both were."

Tessie Collender brings in cheese and crackers, worries with Elizabeth about cookies whose smell is in the air. John Bach comes in and Sister Julie De Femina. With Jesuit Father Ned Murphy and the Berrigans, they make up the nonviolent-resistance community of Jonah House. This is a sharing community, patterned after that of the primitive church. The members pool everything in a common fund and supply all needs from that. All of them are working with groups who are interested in the growth of nonviolent-resistance communities. On weekends the Baltimore group comes together to discuss the work of the week, to share problems, share growth dimensions, deal with aspects of their own life together. It is in this setting that the Christmas Day morality play at the White House was created. Elizabeth speaks of the perfect applicability of the strategy: the medieval Coventry morality plays were themselves aimed at contemporary figures. Hence King Herod — Richard Nixon. The faces were those of actual victims, so they used the faces of wounded and dead Vietnamese children. The broken dolls symbolized the mutilated bodies of the babies Herod had killed and the babies the U.S. had napalmed. I think of the Harrisburg trial, the months Phil Berrigan was incarcerated in Danbury, how the enormous charisma of these two people animates and strengthens this tiny center of resistance. I ask Elizabeth if she is critical of religious life. And I surprise a flash of resentment.

"I'm not going to accept that formulation — that I'm critical of contemporary religious life. Not in the sense that some people are trying to foist it on me. Because I'm not. I think there's a lot of potentiality there and a lot of hope there. I've got questions about people in it and what seems to be the way they live, they value it. In many cases it looks like it's become upper-middle-class life-style by and large. That in spite of all kinds of goodwill. And I'm critical of that. Critical of holding onto certain forms rather than being able to search out others." (She credits the Marymount Sisters with having nurtured and supported her in her antiwar activities.) "They shoved the right books in my direction, the right people. There's a very strong, very fine corps of nuns who were concerned about political issues and involved in them. By and large — to the extent to which there was a split between us, this is where it came from: they were fairly content to deal with the question of peace, the question of justice within the structures, the confines of the class-room or administrative position rather than in any way in the streets. And I'm not saying it shouldn't be dealt with there. I am saying that to keep it there exclusively isn't very helpful or not all that needs to be done."

It is time to catch a train to Washington, so I raise one last question: "Are you hopeful about the possibility of creating a peace movement in this country?"

She grows deeply reflective. She is not sure that it is a possibility. But through multiplication of the kind of nonviolent community they have in Baltimore, people's *attitudes* will be affected. So when the time for organizing a movement comes, there will be many people ready for it.*

Riding back to Washington, I try to fit all the pieces of this little mosaic together. Philip Berrigan calls Elizabeth "a true resistance woman." And that is precisely how she comes across: assured, strong, but obviously one-half of a team. She doesn't think their present form of community at Jonah House will replace other forms of religious life. But it is an alternative. Even bringing up children in this community will be a freeing experience all the way around —

---

* Interview with the author, Baltimore, January 5, 1974.

far more so than in the nuclear family where parents have virtually become slaves to their children. Here there are others to share the pleasure and care of the child, others to enrich a child as well.

Is it a religious community? Without question. Its noncanonical status seems to me singularly unimportant. Because it is risky, it will have few imitators. But Jonah House may well prove to be one of the most significant innovations for the Church in America. A new growth, discontinuous with traditional religious life, it is really a throwback to earlier noncelibate forms of Christian community. It is radical, not in the sense of veering toward the left, but in the sense of going back to the root of primitive Christian life.

In her own terms, Sister Elizabeth McCormack is not a bit avant-garde. In fact, she declares, fixing me with a pair of singularly penetrating blue eyes, "I'm an old-fashioned nun. Either that or nothing at all." It's her word and I have to accept it, but it's an incongruous label for one of the more creative educators on the national scene. When Ms. McCormack announced that she was resigning from Manhattanville College in Purchase, New York ("I'd had eight years as president and seven before that at the college; I felt I'd given all I could offer"), she was asked if she was planning to leave the Society. "Because the previous president had stayed in office till she was sixty-nine and the one preceding her had died in office. Since I really *was* thinking about it, I decided just to bite the bullet and do it." Making the decision was extraordinarily difficult. "But once I'd done it, extraordinarily easy."

And why, after thirty years, did she so decide?

"The decision to leave is always on many levels," she replies crisply. And on one level, she thinks the Society in its present form (in fact, religious life) is "going out of business. When your resources are limited, you should *concentrate* them if they're to be

effective at all. But just the opposite seems to me to be happening."
She gestures eloquently. "Instead of concentrating resources, the
options for individuals, for religious communities, and for congregations are wider and wider. For example, I could have remained
a Religious of the Sacred Heart and worked at the Rockefeller
Brothers Fund. One can say, 'If the Spirit is leading me, I should
go there.'" She snorts delicately. "I don't believe the group makes
any sense at all then." She can't see a group of twenty-five nuns
scattering into twenty-five different jobs. "The fact that we are a
group working together has a greater impact. That's not the modern
thinking. I'm very old-fashioned."

"But certainly you are not opposed to change?"

"No. We were an extremely rigorous group which *had* to change.
As a member of our 1967 Chapter, I was able to be influential. We
had to change in virtue of the needs of the world we were serving.
We were serving that world through the work of education. And
community was a function of that apostolate."

I see the crux of the problem. "Now," I suggest, "community is
central and not peripheral. It seems to be focusing more on itself."

"Yes. To have one's 'apostolate' subject to life in community, is,
in my opinion, a backward step. It isn't that we cannot do the work;
it is that we as a group have decided *not* to do it. So the religious
congregation as a human institution, as I see it, no longer makes
sense. And if one's personal religious position is changing at the
same moment that the thrust for the good of man seems to be
dissipated, then it makes sense on no level."

"You think it has no future?"

"The basic question is — can a total institution which puts
demands on people survive when the structure disappears and no
new structure is substituted?"

"That's a question only time is going to answer for us, I think."

"And if it can, it's because in *fact* it's not a natural grouping. It's really supernatural in the old meaning of that word." *

It's a point of view — and not a popular one. But it is backed by good, hard, rational argument. One can only admire the courage it takes to stand by it. But this is no woman to polish up the brass on the Titanic! It is easy to see why Manhattanville has moved into a prestigious position among private liberal arts colleges. The Rockefellers' gain is the Society's loss.

And where, I wonder, do I locate *myself* between the polar positions these two Elizabeths occupy? One who sees the life as a highly viable option; one who sees it as no option whatever. Right in the middle, I have to admit. Viable — but not for me.

Why, in the end, did I leave religious life? Mainly because I had come to realize that I had grown into quite another person from the twenty-two-year-old girl who once felt compelled to "follow a vocation" and dedicate myself to Catholic education. Today I am convinced that God has really no plan for me other than the one I evolve for myself. Since I feel able to grow more fully as a person outside the structure of religious life, then that is His will for me. Nor do I think, as once I did, that the survival of Catholic education is tied to the voluntary services of nuns. For the best interests of all concerned, nuns should be fully compensated as professional women and free to make whatever contribution they wish to whatever causes they choose. Moreover, it is no longer clear to me that the educational enterprise outranks the needs of the impoverished, the imprisoned, the politically oppressed. I am strongly in favor of nuns going into politics, running for community offices, working in the public sector. This diversity may well effect their

* Interview with the author, New York City, March 26, 1974.

diaspora by integrating them into the larger community and at times leading them back into secular life. What matters, however, is not that we never change a commitment, but that it remain meaningful, growth-producing. When this is no longer the case, one must have the courage to move on.

So it was with me. When, during months of honest self-scrutiny, I unraveled the skein of my own convictions, I at last could find no raison d'etre for me in religious life. My decision to leave had little to do with my doctrinal beliefs. Admittedly, I do not, as once I did, buy bag and baggage the whole of the Catholic creed. (There are moments in the Liturgy when I fall intermittently silent.) I have grave reservations as to official Church positions on significant moral and ethical issues. The matter of the Pope's infallibility is a nonquestion for me. And I long ago lost what vestigial anthropomorphic notions I had of God. Technically, I would, I suppose, be labeled a heretic. Yet for me Christianity remains the single most hopeful, most rewarding way of life.

But to step outside the legal structures of religious life is not to lose any of these dimensions. One's values do not suddenly evaporate. I suppose that I shall always be an unacquisitive person, fond of a simple life, in need of close human relationships, obsessed with the search for transcendental meaning. To leave is to free oneself of certain legalities, to lose a public image with all its built-in expectations, to open oneself again to that beautiful, varied universe one once declined. If you are very young, the journey back to the crossroads to pick up the main-traveled highway is presumably neither long nor arduous. In the afternoon of your life, you have a lot of second thoughts about backtracking. But if in the end it seems worth the risks involved, you make an about-face.

I remember that I told my sister Marion first. "Well, I never wanted you to go from the start," she reminded me laconically. "But

I'm glad you're telling me: I'll change my will." And she kissed me like a little sister again.

I was to sign my papers in the vicar's office on August 10, and I thanked whatever weather gods came up with that sunny, incredibly beautiful morning. I needed all the support I could get against the antiseptically precise little ceremony one goes through at exit. No clouds of incense, no golden Gregorian chants mark these rites of passage. The vicar's office (rather fittingly, I thought) is tucked away in the higher reaches of the Dental Building on Chicago Avenue. Across a totally empty Lemon-Pledged desk, the "papers" are placed before you. There is one last chance to change your mind. Then you are reminded that the congregation you are leaving owes you nothing legally. In *charity,* it will provide a small sum to keep me off the streets lest I prove an embarrassment to the Church. (Father Mulvihill solemnly recounts a harrowing episode involving an unfortunate seventeenth-century ex-nun whose desperate poverty had driven her into an even older profession at the very door of the cathedral.) At my stricken look, he quickly reassures me. Canon law now sees to it that the congregation in *charity* —"In *justice,*" I insist. But it's a losing battle. Father gently reminds me of his doctorate in canon law and, sensing a dissertation panting in the wings and about to pop out, I hastily withdraw from the fray. Charity or no, I sign my name. And it is over.

Downstairs Donatus is idling the motor in the No Parking zone. A sharp glance and she offers to buy me a drink to mark my "coming out." But instead we drive home beside the insanely sparkling lake, already outlining a campaign to get a woman into the office of vicar. We all had served Chicken Simla for dinner that night. Or was it standing rib? There was a good wine, I remember, and candles, and an irreverent replay of the "Exit Interview" and a marvelous flow of novitiate stories. It was a good night.

The warm concern and support of one's community ("Don't look for an apartment right away. We'll help you find something smashing. Let's finish out the lease together") — these rob the moment of official separation of the trauma it once held. The day of the "spoiled nun" hidden away in her mother's back bedroom is over. Thank God for that. No one any longer packs a little black bag in the middle of the night, calls a taxi at dawn, and, like a Dreiser heroine, disappears to surface years later in some distant city. Still, *The Nun's Story* did not exaggerate for its time. Things went just that way when to leave meant to defect. The name was erased; the book was closed. Prayers for "the grace of perseverence" were intensified.

When I think about the future of religious life now, I think that for a long time communities are going to remain small. As the sexist orientation of the Catholic Church becomes increasingly clear to them, women will enter in fewer numbers. Yet I am sure that celibate life will continue to attract some who feel a bonding with others in the sisterhood of liberation. And conventual life may become the locus for a concerted attack on the carefully guarded male citadel of ordination. Candidates entering novitiates today frequently admit that they have an eye on the priesthood.

Nuns in the future will also be far less clerically dominated. "Father" will *not* know best! And nuns will turn more and more to each other for insight, support, spiritual encouragement. Even the Jesuits may find themselves looking for work as nuns take over and give spiritual direction to their own members. (To paraphrase Sissy Farenthold, it is time for incompetent nuns to join incompetent priests in the giving of annual retreats!) There is a rising sense of frustration over having to "find" a priest to celebrate the Liturgy whenever nuns come together for community meetings. More and more they will, I feel, opt for paraliturgical services and the sharing of hosts already consecrated. The increased use of nuns to administer the Eucharist, to preach homilies, and to serve as chaplains will intensify the demand for ordination. As never before, I predict that nuns will ask "Why?"

Why should male pastors "run" parish schools? Why should male superintendents administer diocesan school systems in which women teachers predominate? Why should nuns consult male psychologists and doctors if women are available? Why must women religious confess to celibate men who traditionally have joked about the mild peccadillos of nuns and then imposed harsh penances for "feminine" weakness they profess not to understand? Why must women studying theology be relegated to Regina Mundi, much as Harvard once relegated women to Radcliffe College? Why not women priests, bishops, cardinals? Why not a woman Pope? (The ecclesiastical styles are made for them!) Why is God "He"? Why sexual at all, since not made in our human image but totally transcending and transforming it?

Thanks to the women's revolution gathering momentum in today's society, women entering conventual life will tend to be "whole" persons who have shaken off the stereotypical characteristics of their predecessors. Once pliant, withdrawn, sexless, nuns will emerge as strong, assertive, rational, affectively alive persons with a positive self image. They will see themselves differently in relation to other women, to men, to God. Certainly the "Bride of Christ" metaphor will be dead for them, its sexist overtones having made it totally unacceptable. Their vocations will be to the world and its manifold problems. To solve these, they will reach out for the power, strength, and influence they need, addressing themselves to the entire range of society, not exclusively to the wants of children and the old.

When I think about the future of religious life, I think, too, that leaving it may come to be the norm, not the exception. I suspect that impermanence — entering for two, three, five years — may be more typical than not. And I like to think that in my congregation I have done my part to normalize separation. Staying on at Pratt Avenue, rejoining the faculty at Mundelein — both had symbolic value, I'm certain. What this said was, "I'm still me. I've just changed my way of specifying my Christian commitment." There are discontinuities, to be sure, but the essential continuity of person remains. In class, the kids slip or forget or don't know, and say "Sister." Salespeople at Winsberg's department store still say archly, "You're a nun, aren't you? Don't tell *me*. I always know." And I do not disabuse such canny perceptiveness. Besides, even I catch myself saying, "We BVM's." I'm an associate member of Region 10 in the congregation. I attend a regionally sponsored consciousness-raising session in which nuns and laywomen together are coming to realize that, like Rosie O'Grady and the Colonel's Lady, we're sisters under the skin. If theologian Mary Daly is right, the awareness of their common oppression will yet unite women across all creedal and social divisions in a single sisterhood of undreamed strength.

It is in such developments as Region 10 that I sense something new stirring in traditional American religious life. This is an experimental region of BVM's formed about eighteen months ago at the Chicago grass-roots level. It is made up of like-minded people, more process-oriented than most, interested in free dialogical exchange as a method of discovering corporate thrust. Mary De Cock was elected to head up that region. When I ask her why a new region was necessary before the new governmental structures are even five years old, her explanation is characteristically political.

"Well, in retrospect, it was really a criticism of the democratic process. We had created a democratic government for the congregation as a whole — evolutionary and self-correcting, as we put it. But five years after it went in we found it so cumbersome that it couldn't work. So we got together a group of people who wanted to let change happen without trying to program it. Canon lawyers like to say that life precedes law. But in a predominantly Irish, Jesuitical, rationalistic group such as the BVM's have historically been, we tend to want to blueprint evolution. We're so scientifically minded that we have to have an evaluative structure set up before we can risk an experiment! So we talk about the risk of radical Gospel living, but we try to filter out any possibility of the risk of failure. And what you have at that point is frequently neither radical nor Gospel."

"How good are the chances that something new will evolve out of the traditional religious orders?"

"It's hard to tell. The Constitution on the Church in the Modern World spoke of the necessity for fresh forms arising to meet new needs. But I've always found that part of the document weak. It seemed to foreclose the possibility that present forms of religious life could themselves evolve to meet new needs. I'd like to think this is possible. In Region 10 we've created a structure to facilitate this. But, I have to admit —" she grins and shrugs —"it's damned slow going!"

"Because you have to pull the whole congregation along with you as you try to evolve?"

"Not really. But we do constantly have to be looking in both directions — on the one hand to problems of ministry, on the other to problems of internal relations. So our energies are constantly divided. If we set out to work for social change, we have to cover all the bases on the administrative board ahead of time to make sure our proposals aren't axed. We can't seem to get so far away from the group that we're rejected. We have to stay in dialogue."

I learn that 15 to 20 percent of Region 10 members are individually committed to a wide range of causes. They are working for the Alliance to End Repression, for the United Farm Workers, Alcoholics Anonymous, the Illinois Crime Commission, the Urban Apostolate; they're involved in community organization, pastoral counseling in hospitals, a variety of parish ministries.

"What about the peace movement?"

"Right now, a group of BVM's — most of them members of the region — is working to establish a Center for Peace and Justice in Chicago. This is an intercongregational attempt to avoid duplication of effort by zeroing in on specific problems in various parts of the country. One center might focus on the problems of farm workers, another on the issue of amnesty, another on corporate investment of Church organizations. It occurs to me that such a center in the Chicago area could also serve as a focus for the region. At the moment our efforts are pretty diffused and uncoordinated. I guess that's one of the undesirable side effects of so much freedom. There isn't a very pervasive sense of cohesion, of group thrust, though there is a small core of perhaps thirty or forty people working toward this. We can't marshal our forces from the top any more, neither in the congregation-at-large nor in the region. We're so busy enjoying our 'freedom from' that we haven't yet learned how to harness together our 'freedoms for' and make them count."

"And what about community life? Is there pressure toward new forms — toward mixed communities, for instance?"

"It's certainly been discussed. In Region 10 no idea is too radical to be talked about! But the possibility of this happening soon is extremely remote. Probably because we've lost so many of the young who might be pushing for this. No, the only 'mixing' Region 10 members are doing is with a few nuns from other orders or with their own former members." She waves her Tareyton in my direction. "Like you, for example!"

Our conversation turns to the effect of having "outsiders" in the consciousness-raising sessions. We agree that such women are helpful to politicize the group in the direction of serious involvement in the struggle for liberation. A realist of the first rank, she concedes that "we may not be around to see it. But women are dead certain to come into their own. And nuns can do a lot to make it happen. In fact right in the Church is where we may do our best work. That's one of the ironic things about a congregation like ours that's very sensitive to canon law and to working within the structure. Eventually you realize that you've got to change the Church before you can tackle the problems of the world."

"You think it's worth the effort?"

"Sometimes I wonder. But then I realize that, after all, the Church is a big chunk of the world. And, in view of that fact, the ordination of women might just be the greatest contribution we could make toward the liberation of women generally." *

With people like Mary De Cock on hand to analyze the issues and help develop viable strategies of response, Region 10 seems likely seed ground for creative change within the BVM congregation. There is discussion just now about opening up BVM living groups to young women who want to experience community on a short-term basis. Not with the expectation of joining the order. Just to share the riches, the human dimension of a Christian community that is alive and supportive and concerned about making a difference in society. The BVM's may yet sponsor "fresh forms to meet new needs."

* Interview with the author, Chicago, May 18, 1974.

Actually, some congregations of nuns have already opened their doors to allow others to share the life of the community. The Dominican Sisters in Racine, Wisconsin, have developed an associate program to facilitate temporary relationships between the community and young women who want the experience of living in a faith community for a time. The Benedictines at St. Joseph, Minnesota, run a similar program with a focus on volunteer service. The Milwaukee Franciscans include married people and priests among their associates. Though hardly radical, these are tentative steps away from the exclusionist character which has thus far marked American orders. Such moves implicitly recognize the need for a wide range of religious expression. And once the ice is broken, it will be hard to draw the line.

In Sainte-Baume (France) a far more novel community includes Dominican priests, contemplative Dominican nuns, and five married couples with ten children. All have come together with a desire for a richer spiritual life. "They no longer felt at ease in the traditional forms of the Church," says their director, Father Maillard, "and they saw coming here as a means of going forward." There are innumerable problems to be solved in dealing with such a mixed group — male, female, celibate and married, vowed and salaried personnel. But such a microcosm has to have a human dimension sex-segregated societies cannot claim.

This need for a more human mode of life, it seems to me, accounts for the understanding of the vow of chastity current among some young religious who tend to speak by preference of a vow of celibacy. And this vow they strictly delimit as positing a state of not being married, not instituting a family, being free from the institutional and legal status which binds, without rigidly excluding from one's life deep and affectionate human relationships.

On the other hand, Jesuit Father Nick Conolly, campus minister at Canisius College, Buffalo, feels that one vows a virtue, not a state in life. And that chastity is a call to deep, clear love: *just* love. He dissociates from this virtue overtones of negativity and repression which arise out of the opposition of the traditional dualisms: body-soul, sacred-profane, matter-spirit, God-woman. Though spirit-love is often construed to be love without body, he sees perfect love as spirit in body and stresses the necessity of seeking new understandings of sexuality, affectivity, and friendship in the light of celibate ministry. For Father Conolly, what celibacy says essentially is that the ministry of Jesus is absolutely prior to any other concern, whether project or person. And he points out that this ought to be true of every Christian, married or not. "At the heart of any deep, significant friendship between a man and a woman, whether married or close friends in celibate ministry, the invitation is the same: to find in their mutual love the grounding of God's presence which launches each one into ministry. All true love is creative, though not always procreative as in marriage."

To contrast this description of celibate love with the frigid language of my Rule regarding chastity ("Never for the shortest space of time shall they be alone with a man. . . .") is to realize afresh the biological determinism, the morbid mistrust of sexuality which underlay such a principle of conduct. The young are wiser than we in their generation. They recognize celibate love as a gift, and deeply spiritual. "Touch can be sacramental," as Nick observes. "The expression of affection is chaste when it releases the joy, the prayer, and the love energy to discover God's presence and live with his will. Energy for preaching, desire for service in ministry are congruent to the truly significant and beautiful friendships with which ministers of the word of Jesus are blessed."

Such a point of view is founded on a rich understanding of

person and of the unremitting need for human interchange if growth is to be nurtured. It demands very careful distinctions, for the matter is far more complicated than can be described in traditional either-or terms: celibacy or marriage. The deep friendship Father Conolly refers to is characterized by a sense of purpose and honesty. And those involved in it must rely on their faith and their hope, as well as their love, to discover the freedom to respond to the friendship at all its depths. "I know from experience," he asserts, "that ministry can only benefit by such special friends — gifts from the Father." *

Rewarding as such a friendship has to be, for other young people leading celibate lives it is not enough. The need for mutual human support has led to marriage itself, though marriage within the context of the community. Where this has happened, the marriage is looked upon as one of common consent outside of civil law, one not requiring separation from the religious group. A faculty member at Union Theological Seminary described to me one such relationship which involved a friend of hers (a Protestant girl) and a Catholic Brother. During the wedding ceremony the two exchanged promises in the presence of a few friends and the assembled religious community. Although not an ordained priest, the newly married Brother then offered a Liturgy of celebration (omitting the Consecration). To bring in a priest from outside the community would have seemed an intrusion on its privacy.

I was intrigued. "He was not the first to do this, then?"

"Apparently not. As there was no marriage license, there is no legal relationship. The Brother is still under vows. Eventually the group hopes to establish a mixed community."

* Personal letter to the author, undated, 1974.

This situation suggests how life precedes law, making changes quietly, incrementally, and in this case implicitly suggesting new directions for religious life in the future.

Though "mixed community" remains still on the distant horizon for most canonical groups in America, it has become a reality for the Immaculate Heart Community of Los Angeles which, after a stormy battle with Cardinal McIntyre, in 1970 became a secular community without official ties to the Church. To Margaret Rose Whelan, president of the community, the fact that celibacy is now optional is a major plus. "If you choose to live a celibate life when you don't have to in order to belong fully to the group, you look very carefully at your motivation." In this regard, most members feel that they are living more authentically than ever before.

"The members can marry, then?"

"Yes. Most of the approximately two hundred and twenty members have remained celibate. But last year two of those members decided to marry. And in both cases the husbands are not members of the community." * But in no way, it is felt, has this new commitment lessened that to the community. Four years after the most anguished period in its history, the group has a clear sense of its own identity, a deep commitment to exploring the mystery of God and to sharing the Gospel message of peace. Diversifying its membership has been one of its richest experiences.

The Immaculate Heart Community, mixed and secular; the Jonah House community, resistant-nonviolent — these represent something radically new to American Catholicism. Yet each of these new forms has evolved from the most traditional kind of religious institutes and is rooted in essential Christian values: belief in the Gospel imperative, the centrality of community, commitment to

* Interview with the author, Washington, D.C., August, 1974.

peacemaking. In both communities the dimension of human caring is at stage center. Both are furthering the life-giving values of their members, free of the hassles the official Church can create.

Neither group, I'm sure, sees itself as replacing other forms of religious life. But they offer alternative models which are persuasive and attractive. And they may well turn out to be important shaping influences on the future Church in America.

Will religious life survive into the the twenty-first century? It's anybody's guess. Certainly it is beset by dangers. There is the danger that, immersed in the world, nuns may imperceptibly begin to reflect rather than resist the pervasive cultural values which surround them. "They're free to work where they want, free to do what they think they should," admits Margaret Whelan. "We have to work to bring about an interior conversion, a raising of consciousness. We can't invoke the structure any more. It doesn't exist." *

There is the danger too that there will develop a great pressure for a "return to normality"— an effort to put everybody back into a set of boxes again, *new*, but boxes still. To expert Vatican watchers, the Third International Synod (Rome, 1971) really shifted to the right of Vatican II, to the right of contemporary theology and Biblical scholarship.[1] Certainly this is true in terms of priestly celibacy and the ordination of women. And there are signs that, having rejected the old moral and religious rigidities, some congregations are trying hard to invent new ones. The struggle for change is extraordinarily difficult. Efforts to introduce really radical change, like mixed communities, will face strenuous opposition, and so must be conducted with enormous discretion, even sub rosa (like Brothers who are marrying without benefit of clergy or law).

Yet, the struggle will go on; for the Church will change. It will,

* *Ibid.*
† See Richard McBrien in the *Catholic Messenger*, January 24, 1974.

I am convinced, modify its teaching and its practices on divorce and remarriage, on euthanasia, birth control, abortion, and sexuality. The Church *must* become more deeply committed to the practice as well as the teaching of contemporary morality. It must intensify its focus on societal evils and attack these with every political and legislative tool in addition to its vast moral authority. And the Church must, finally, right the wrongs done to women and admit them to both the priesthood and the episcopacy. All in time. But these things will come.

And they will come in great part, I am certain, because the leadership and the drive to make them happen will emerge out of deeply charismatic, radically Christian communities, canonical or not. Sooner or later most people weary of moral indignation. But a significant minority continue the aggressive fight for peace and justice. Around these stern prophets will form communities on fire with their vision. These groups will be smaller. They will be mixed. They will be impermanent. They will be risky. And they will be enormously rewarding places to be.